New Land, North of the Columbia

HISTORIC DOCUMENTS THAT TELL THE STORY of WASHINGTON STATE FROM TERRITORY TO TODAY

Lorraine McConaghy

SASQUATCH BOOKS
SEATTLE

Printed in China
Published by Sasquatch Books

15 14 13 12 11   9 8 7 6 5 4 3 2 1

Cover illustration: Columbia Basin Project Map, courtesy of the Shafer Museum, Winthrop, Washington
Cover design: Anna Goldstein
Interior design: Anna Goldstein and Sarah Plein
Interior composition: Sarah Plein

Library of Congress Cataloging-in-Publication Data is available.

ISBN-13: 978-1-57061-693-8

Sasquatch Books
119 South Main Street, Suite 400
Seattle, WA 98104
(206) 467-4300
www.sasquatchbooks.com
custserv@sasquatchbooks.com

Contents

Introduction

This book in your hands presents a journey through the history of Washington State and its peoples over time, shown by a wide-ranging selection of the documents preserved in the state's archives, large and small. This magnificent common treasury of file folders, microfilm reels, and digitized scans records our shared past—housing treaties and patent drawings, political cartoons and FBI files, personal correspondence and business records. There are many possible pathways through this material and many possible journeys—this book represents one historian's selection of documents, each of which tells a story and altogether tell a powerful anthology of stories, situated along a pathway that ends where we are standing right now, in the twenty-first century.

This place we today call "Washington" is Indian ground. Back in 1846, "Washington" became part of the United States when the boundary dispute with Great Britain was settled, dividing Oregon Country between English and American ownership at the 49th parallel. Two years afterward, Oregon Territory was organized, including present-day Washington, Oregon, Idaho, and parts of Montana and Wyoming. Then, in 1853, Washington settlers successfully concluded their campaign to separate Washington Territory—the new land north of the Columbia—from Oregon Territory, and here the stories of this book begin.

We can follow a paper trail from the territory's very founding with President Franklin Pierce's appointment of his political cronies to the patronage jobs of the new territory: governor, secretary, surveyor-general, Indian agents, and so on down the line. Federal and state archives hold the territory's

early documents: the act of Congress creating the territory; resolutions of the territorial legislature; treaties with Native people; maps and charts; railroad surveys; and correspondence among territorial officials, and between them and their superiors in Washington, DC—"Washington City," as it was then called.

As the territory grew through the 1870s and 1880s, the long-awaited completion of the transcontinental railroad through to Puget Sound spurred anticipation of statehood. The railroad offered migrants an easier route than the long cross-country trail, and it also opened distant markets to Washington products: coal, timber, fish, and wheat. With a growing population and strong resource-based economy, residents could confidently anticipate recognition of the territory's maturity. And in 1889, Washington finally became a state.

After statehood, Washington's unfolding stories grow increasingly diverse and complex, but the paper trail continues. The United States government played a powerful role in the state's development, administering tribal reservations; distributing land to settlers; collecting revenue; counting residents; issuing patents; naturalizing new citizens; building forts, shipyards, and bases; setting aside federal land for parks, grazing, and forests; accomplishing the state's dramatic New Deal transformation; and building a wide variety of military bases. Washington's residents elected a host of men and women to govern them, and they in turn generated state, county, and municipal agencies to oversee the state's franchise, morals, loyalty, health, education, transportation, and industrial and agricultural development. Oversight of these activities generated documents—everything from quarantine resolutions to cattle and log brand records, marriage certificates to mug shots.

Washington folks also wrote diaries, postcards, and letters; posed for photos; sent birthday and holiday cards; sketched their homes; crafted poetry; and made music. They went to work and attended schools; worshipped together; and joined clubs, labor unions, and political parties. They were laid off and went on the dole; they headed to work and paid their taxes; they went to war on the homefront or they sailed away to distant war; and they read newspapers and chuckled at political cartoons. When they went out to lunch, they chose their meal from menus; at the market, they bought brightly labeled Washington products. All of these activities left paper trails for us to follow, together.

For nearly a year, I traveled to archives throughout Washington State to search for the documents I thought you would like to see. The documents had to be generated after 1853 within the place we today call Washington State, and held in archives and libraries accessible to the public. Occasionally, I moved beyond a doctrinaire definition of "archival," to bring a published but out-of-print document before you that seemed particularly significant. As a historian, I view these documents as primary evidence of who we have been and who we are, and perhaps who we might one day become. These documents tie us to times and places in the past; they inform the narrative of Washington's history; they point the way to the future.

As I leaf through this book, every document has its own story—the archivist who went above and beyond to find a promising collection, the technical difficulties of making a particular scan, the satisfaction of finding just the right thing, the pleasure of pulling documents together to explore a topic, and the delight of discovery. I first ran across the map that documents the Native geography of the Olympia area as a poor photocopy, and months later traced it to the hand-drawn original. I couldn't believe that Abraham Lincoln wrote his own telegram to our governor—and signed it! I was

thrilled to find Theodore Roethke's rough draft of "The Rose," the poem he read to great acclaim at Century 21. I held a beat-up green register in my hand, and opened it to find page after page of ecstatic testimony scrawled by climbers at the very summit of Mount Rainier. Above all, I think, the two dozen faces in this book are deeply moving. Whether they are seen in mug shots or portraits, they convey to me our shared human experience, here in this place.

This book represents a work in progress, work that can never be completed. At times I thought of this project as a fool's errand because it was impossible for me to visit all the collections that deserved inclusion, impossible for me to master the hundreds of thousands of linear feet of documents at the three dozen places I *did* visit. It proved difficult even to communicate the scope of this project, for which there were no focused research questions. Instead, I was asking to see the documents that would concentrate a great deal of Washington history in one page; documents that were easily legible; documents that were beautiful, amusing, powerful, or even dangerous. As I visited archives large and small, from Bellingham to the Tri-Cities, Newport to Kelso, I imagined you sitting beside me as I read through file folders and combed through boxes. Of the huge range of possibilities, what would you choose?

Myself, I chose hundreds of documents, more than three times as many as you see in this book. One morning when I walked into my study, the walls were no longer visible because of the photocopies and scans taped to the bookshelves. So in the end, I simply had to stop and choose the selection of documents that you see before you. The digitization of records has made it possible to quickly search some collections online by date and keyword, to find the handful of documents that match set criteria. While I am grateful for that ease, I hope that this book encourages a different kind of research.

"Finding" the digitized documents that include the words "Stevens" plus "Leschi" is no substitute for browsing the folders that include and give context to those documents. Although this book provides citations, it was never my intent to enable you to leap to the individual document, but rather to encourage you to visit the archive yourself and ask to browse the collection. That's why we preserve this material—so future generations can explore the records in their full context. I hope that this book will inspire you to ask your own questions of our magnificent shared archival collection of Washington territorial and state history, and to value the work of those who care for that collection.

—Lorraine McConaghy,
Seattle 2011

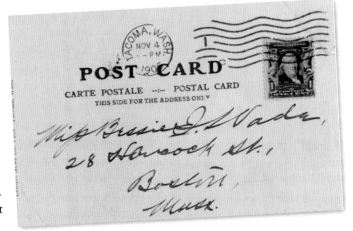

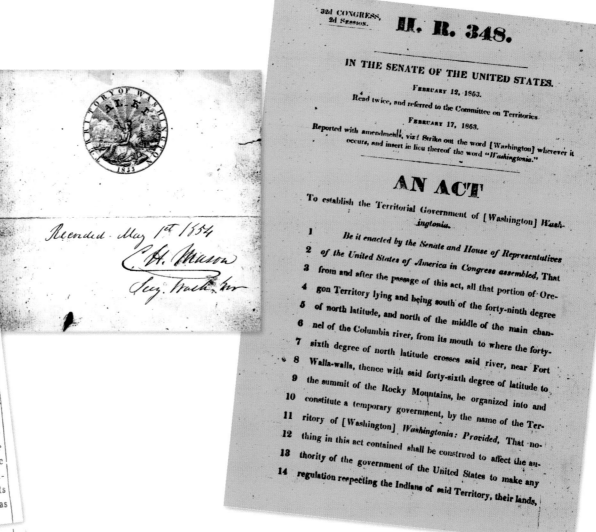

THE COLUMBIAN.

OLYMPIA, PUGET SOUND, O. T.

Saturday, October 16, 1852.

What Northern Oregon Wants.

Well, what does she want?—what will she need?—and what require?

She wants the assembling of a convention at some suitable point within the territory, and that too, as early as practicable, to take the necessary steps towards the creation of a NEW TERRITORY, north of the Columbia. She wants as many families of this year's immigration as CAN, to join our settlements this fall. She wants steamers on the Sound—steam mills, and all other kinds of machinery established throughout the territory—a distinct understanding among the people, where the route across the Cascade mountains is to be located, and the preliminary measures relative to all these subjects arranged satisfactorily to all, and as soon as possible...

...Citizens of northern Oregon! it behooves you to bestir yourselves, and proclaim your independence of the territorial authority exerted over you by the Willamette valley. Call meetings in your several precincts; memorialize congress to set us off; exhibit our grievances both in omission and commission under which we have suffered from ALL departments of government, and that body will be COMPELLED to regard your prayer.

Recorded May 1st 1854

C. H. Mason

Sec. Wash. Ter.

H. R. 348.

32d CONGRESS,
2d Session.

IN THE SENATE OF THE UNITED STATES.

FEBRUARY 12, 1853.

Read twice, and referred to the Committee on Territories.

FEBRUARY 17, 1853.

Reported with amendments, viz: Strike out the word [Washington] wherever it occurs, and insert in lieu thereof the word "Washingtonia."

AN ACT

To establish the Territorial Government of [Washington] Washingtonia.

1 Be it enacted by the Senate and House of Representatives
2 of the United States of America in Congress assembled, That
3 from and after the passage of this act, all that portion of Ore-
4 gon Territory lying and being south of the forty-ninth degree
5 of north latitude, and north of the middle of the main chan-
6 nel of the Columbia river, from its mouth to where the forty-
7 sixth degree of north latitude crosses said river, near Fort
8 Walla-walla, thence with said forty-sixth degree of latitude to
9 the summit of the Rocky Mountains, be organized into and
10 constitute a temporary government, by the name of the Ter-
11 ritory of [Washington] Washingtonia: Provided, That no-
12 thing in this act contained shall be construed to affect the au-
13 thority of the government of the United States to make any
14 regulation respecting the Indians of said Territory, their lands,

GETTING STARTED—BECOMING A TERRITORY

The Olympia *Columbian*—the first newspaper published north of the Columbia River—went to press in September 1852 to agitate for the separation of "northern Oregon" from Oregon Territory. The *Columbian*'s campaign was successful, and we see the U.S. Senate's enabling legislation for "Washingtonia," in February of 1853. Once Washington Territory was hastily renamed and established, federal appointees were dispatched to the far West to govern the huge new territory, and they began to create the bureaucratic paper trail housed by the Washington State Archives. The territorial seal shown here adopted the Chinook trading jargon phrase "al-ki"—or "in a little while"—to demonstrate confidence in Washington Territory's rapid transition from prairie schooners and log cabins to steamships and shining cities.

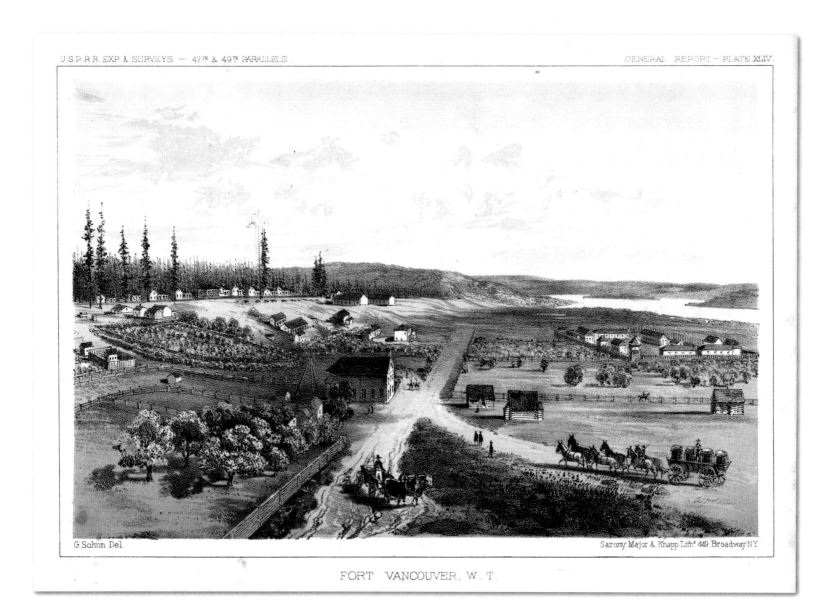

G. Sohon Del.

Sarony Major & Knapp Lith. 449 Broadway NY

FORT VANCOUVER, W. T.

2

FORT VANCOUVER

Isaac Ingalls Stevens was appointed Washington Territory's first governor, a reward by Democratic president Franklin Pierce for Stevens's support during the presidential campaign. Stevens had multiple responsibilities, ranging from concluding treaties with Northwest Native people to surveying the best route across the United States for a northern tier transcontinental railroad. In November 1853, Gustav Sohon sketched this view of Fort Vancouver, the headquarters of the Hudson's Bay Company's Columbia District, later published in Stevens's *United States Pacific Railroad Survey*. Situated on the northern bank of the Columbia River, Fort Vancouver had become much more than just a British fur-trading outpost—it was a little town that included a wooden stockade, homes and storehouses, a school and church, a sawmill and gristmill, a "factory" for processing furs, orchards and gardens, a small shipyard and substantial docks on the river. Many early settlers from back East ended their lengthy journey by land or sea at Fort Vancouver, resting up before heading north.

This is to certify that
David Denny & Louisa
his wife was married
by me a justice of the
peace on the 23rd day
of January AD 1853 at
the house of A. A. Denny
near the town of Seattle in
King County Oregon Terri-
tory in the presence of A. A.
Denny wife & others
D.S. Maynard J.P.
H.L. Yesler
Clerk—

No 1

FIRST KING COUNTY MARRIAGE CERTIFICATE

Seattle was founded on the eastern shore of Elliott Bay in the spring of 1852, and King County was created on December 22, 1852, before Washington Territory even existed. So for a few months letters arrived in Seattle addressed to So-and-So, Seattle, King County, O.T., or Oregon Territory. The county was originally named for Vice President William Rufus King in an effort to curry favor with the administration then in office back in Washington, DC, or "Washington City," as the nation's capital was called in the West. Here we see the first entry in King County's Record of Marriage Certificates, recording the wedding of settlers David Denny and Louisa Boren, on January 23, 1853, accompanied by a veritable parade of Seattle founders. David "Doc" Maynard served as justice of the peace and Henry Yesler as clerk; Arthur and Mary Denny served as witnesses.

POINT ELLIOTT TREATY

The Point Elliott Treaty is a federal document that acknowledges that Washington Territory was Indian ground. Native and government representatives had to sign a contract including a set of agreements that permitted settlers to claim land in the territory in return for promised rights and compensation—a treaty. Governor Isaac Stevens was responsible for concluding these contracts with Native people in the far Northwest as quickly as possible and he raced through the process, "negotiating" ten treaties between December 1854 and January 1856, from Neah Bay to the upper Missouri River. These documents were drafted using boilerplate language, adapted to Northwest geography. The Point Elliott Treaty, excerpted here, was concluded on January 22, 1855, but not ratified for more than four years. The treaty council took place at Mukilteo (meaning "good camping ground" to Native people). Governor Stevens and his entourage conducted hasty and dismissive discussions with men identified as the "chiefs" of their "tribes"—American ideas that were foreign to Native understanding. The treaty released more than 54,000 acres of Native land for settlement, and established the Port Madison, Tulalip, Swinomish, and Lummi reservations. In return, Indian people received the promises highlighted here.

Art. X. The above tribes and bands are desirous to exclude from their reservations the use of ardent spirits, and to prevent their people from drinking the same, and therefore it is provided that any Indian belonging to said tribe who is guilty of bringing liquor into said reservations, or who drinks liquor may have his or her proportion of the annuities withheld from him or her for such time as the President may determine.

Art. XI. The said tribes and bands agree to free all slaves now held by them and not to purchase or acquire others hereafter.

Art. XII. The said tribes and bands further agree not to trade at Vancouver's Island or elsewhere out of the dominions of the United States, nor shall foreign Indians be permitted to reside in their reservations without consent of the Superintendent or Agent.

Art. XIII. To enable the said Indians to remove to and settle upon their aforesaid reservations, and to clear, fence and break up a sufficient quantity of land for cultivation, the United States further agree to pay the sum of fifteen thousand dollars to be laid out and expended under the direction of the President and in such manner as he shall approve.

Art. XIV. The United States further agree to establish at the general agency for the District of Puget's Sound, within one year from the ratification hereof, and to support for a period of twenty years, an agricultural and industrial school, to be free to children of the said tribes and bands in common with those of the other tribes of said district, and to provide the said school with a suitable instructor or instructors, and also to provide a smithy and carpenter's shop & furnish them with the necessary tools, and employ a blacksmith, carpenter and farmer for the like term of twenty years to instruct the Indians in their respective occupations. And the United States finally agree

Executed in the presence of us.

M. T. Simmons
Indian Agent

C. H. Mason
Secy. Wash. Ter.

Benj. F. Shaw
Interpreter

Chas. M. Hitchcock

J. H. Goldsborough

George Gibbs

John H. Scranton

Henry D. Cock

S. S. Ford Junr

Orrington Cushman

Ellis Barnes

Isaac I. Stevens (L. S.)
Govr. & Supt.

Seattle X Chief of the Dwamish & Suquamish tribes (L. S.)

Pat-ka-nam X Chief of the Snoqualmoo, Snohomish & other tribes

Chow-its-hoot X Chief of the Lummi and other tribes (L. S.)

Goliah X Chief of the Skagits and other allied tribes (L. S.)

Kwallattum X or Gen. Pierce Sub Chief of Skagit tribe (L. S.)

S'hootst-hoot X Sub Chief of Snohomish (L. S.)

Snah-talc X or Bonaparte Sub Chief of Snohomish (L. S.)

Squush-um X or The Smoke Sub chief of the Snoqualmoo

TUMWATER FALLS

Navy Lieutenant James Alden commanded the
U.S. survey vessel *Active*, whose officers and crew
were responsible for developing the navigational
charts essential to safe passage in northwest waters.
He was also a gifted artist, and here we see one of
his precise and delicate water colors. Alden drew in
1853 the rushing waters of Tumwater Falls on the
Deschutes River, whose water power first attracted
settlers in 1846 to settle on Native ground—the
falls get their name from the Chinook trading jargon word "tum," meaning heart or spirit. Alden
has captured for us the wild, lovely beauty of early
Washington Territory, and also the river's power,
which would soon be turned to industrial uses.

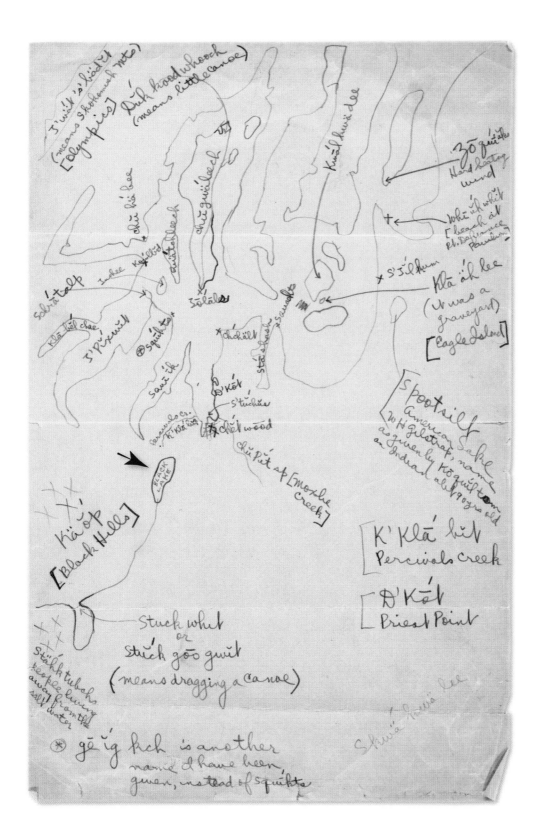

NATIVE GEOGRAPHY OF OLYMPIA AREA

Black Lake helps us get our bearings on this remarkable map of Native place names for the Olympia area. I originally found a photocopy of the map at Washington State Archives and began to hunt for the original. With some good luck, two great archivists, and a lot of time, the original finally turned up in the James Tobin file, Stevens Family Collection, at Washington State Historical Society. Tobin may have been one of Isaac Stevens's treaty translators, and my speculation is that a representative from the Historical Society sat down with Tobin when he was a very old man, perhaps in about 1920, and together they placed these names on this map, delineating a Native geography. Nothing in this anthology more clearly shows that newcomers stand on Native ground.

We whose names are hereunto subscribed, being citizens and Indians of Washington Territory, hereby enlist ourselves and volunteer our services for the purpose of forming a military company to operate against the tribes or bands of hostile Indians now waging war against the United States in said Territory, and hereby agree to serve for ___ month unless sooner discharged.

Olympia. W.T. February 19 1856.

1	Wesley Gosnell		20	Scheuriev
2	Thomas Cambe		21	Bill Jackwood
3	H. D. Morgan	White	22	John Wyhie
4	Thos. S. Mounts		23	Whey-o-has or Jaker
5	Quincy A. Brooks.		24	Ya-tha- or Sam.

Indians
1	Gou-ge-s-bod or Bob.		25	Ti-la-co-las John
2	Ki-ske or Jim		26	Bobra-loo-chie
3	South Bay Jim		27	Skookum Bay Charley
4	Jim McAllister.		28	Cah-s-tel or Bill
5	Quate-wahte-ah or Bill Boxer		29	Je-ells
6	Alla-hewe or Charley		30	Charley Sakeat.
7	Seil-a-coom			
8	Yel-la-lo.			
9	Tsik-co-nim or Doris.			
10	Smah-tau-ak or Charley			
11	Jimmy			
12	Keh-whey			
13	Stel-lole			
14	Mats-m			
15	Skullat			
16	Snohom			
17	Keish			
18	Bill or			
19	Cu-s-ta			

Total of whites and Indians 35.

We expect to be gone two days unless something unforeseen happens.

Yelm Prairie March 30 56

M. Stevens Sir

Indians are coming in and killing cattle, and drivein off horses we would like to have some protection if possible

So I remain your respected

James Longmire

Seattle W.T. Jany. 1856

Methodist Church. · North Blockhouse · Klakunis Tree · Yeslers Mill · Yesler's House · Saw Dust. · Elliot Ho · South Block, Ho. · Made Dammable. Ho.

By Commodore T.S. Phelps U.S.L.

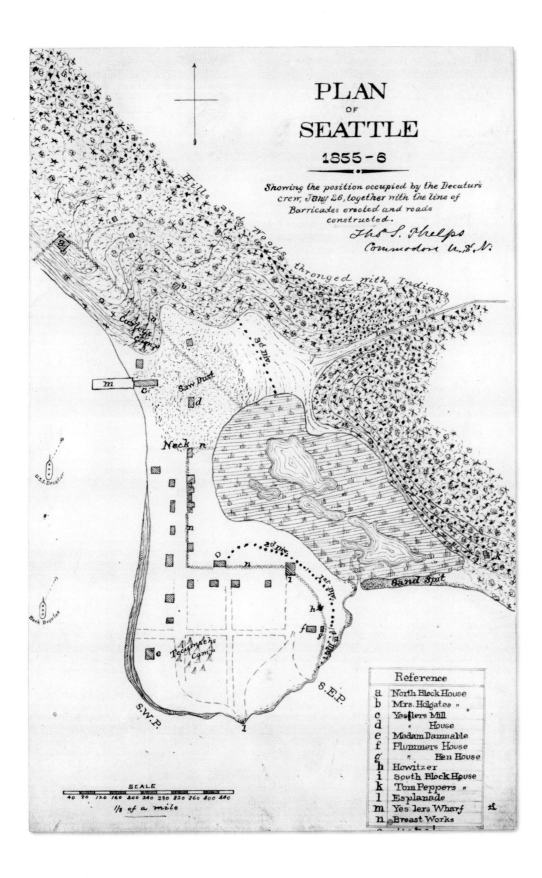

PLAN
OF
SEATTLE
1855–6

Showing the position occupied by the Decatur's
crew, Jany 26, together with the line of
Barricades erected and roads
constructed.

Thos S. Phelps
Commodore U.S.N.

Reference	
a	North Block House
b	Mrs. Holgates "
c	Yeslers Mill
d	" House
e	Madam Dammable
f	Plummers House
g	" Hen House
h	Howitzer
i	South Block House
k	Tom Peppers "
l	Esplanade
m	Yeslers Wharf
n	Breast Works

SCALE
40 80 120 160 200 240 280 320 360 400 440
1/8 of a mile

TREATY WAR

One outcome of Governor Isaac Stevens's hurried treaty making was the subsequent outbreak of the Treaty War in Washington Territory. A growing number of Native people rejected the treaty terms, whose promises went unfulfilled and which confined them to small reservations that did not support their way of life. Tensions grew throughout the spring and summer of 1855, and the territorial legislature sent an anxious appeal back to Washington, DC, requesting federal military protection. On October 14, 1855, Governor Stevens asked Western Washington settlers to enroll in two companies of volunteer militia, and requested arms from a U.S. Navy warship, the *Decatur*, then stationed near in Elliott Bay, off Seattle. The Treaty War had begun, as both sides prepared to fight. Here we see the drawing made of embattled Seattle, attacked on January 26, 1856, by a coalition of Native warriors. Thomas Stowell Phelps, stationed on board the *Decatur*, at anchor in Elliott Bay, made these two sketches that show us the tiny settlement of Seattle. Phelps's extraordinary drawings were later published in his reminiscences, now out of print. Phelps clearly indicated that Seattle's "Hills and Woods [were] Thronged with Indians," along what would today be Second and Third Avenues. We also see James Longmire's scrawled appeal from Yelm, in March of 1856, calling for protection and the enrollment of Native people in the company of "Indian militia" near Olympia.

9

SAN JUAN ISLANDS' PIG WAR

The dispute between Great Britain and the United States over the northern boundary of the Oregon Country was settled in 1846, but uncertainty remained about the division of the San Juan Islands. The map below, published in the San Francisco *Daily Evening Bulletin* on October 28, 1859, shows the two claims very clearly. American settlers and British soldiers lived side by side on San Juan Island, and their uneasy relations were brought to a flash point by a crisis. On June 15, 1859, Lyman Cutlar, an American farmer, was angered to find a pig digging up his garden. Cutlar shot and killed the animal, which belonged to the Hudson's Bay Company. Matters quickly escalated, eventually arraying British warships against American infantry. James Douglas, governor of the Crown Colony of Vancouver's Island, drafted this tart note below to Washington Territory governor Richard Dickerson Gholson, protesting any occupation of San Juan Island by American troops.

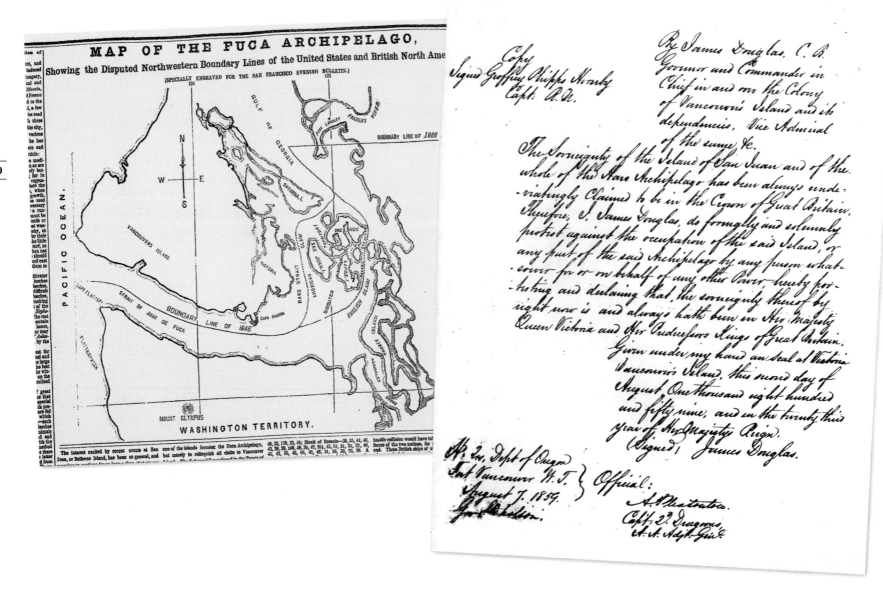

A SLAVE FLEES OLYMPIA

James Tilton was another Democratic Party stalwart, whose allegiance was rewarded by a federal job in Washington Territory. Appointed surveyor-general, Tilton traveled around Cape Horn with his family, an Irish maid, and a young black slave named Charles Mitchell. The group arrived in the territorial capital, Olympia, in March 1855. In 1860 Mitchell was approached by two or three black men from Victoria, who encouraged him to stow away on the steamer *Eliza Anderson* and sail to freedom. On September 26 Mitchell fled his master. Four days later, from Olympia, James Tilton wrote this letter of complaint to Washington Territory's acting governor Henry McGill, protesting the boarding of the *Anderson* at Victoria by British authorities and their seizure of Charles Mitchell. Tilton cast the situation as an unjustifiable violation of United States' rights by Crown Colony civil authorities. But Charles Mitchell remained free in Victoria—the only passenger we know of on the Puget Sound Underground Railroad.

GOVERNOR GHOLSON
GOES SOUTH

Richard Dickerson Gholson was Washington Territory's third governor, appointed by President James Buchanan as a reward for Gholson's political support. A Kentuckian, Gholson owned slaves on his home plantation and also at his extensive ranch in Texas. In the antebellum period, Gholson was vehemently pro-states' rights and pro-slavery. Just prior to Abraham Lincoln's inauguration as president, Gholson penned his resignation to Jeremiah Black, Buchanan's secretary of state. By then Gholson was actively working for the secession of his home state to the newly-formed Confederate States of America. His note indicated that he was "unwilling even for a day to hold office under a (so called) 'Republican' President," but Gholson surely realized that with Lincoln's election, Democratic patronage appointments, like his in Washington Territory, would soon come to an end. In effect, whatever his scruples, Gholson quit before he was fired.

BRIGADIER GENERAL I. INGALLS STEVENS.

Death of General Stevens.

On the outside of this issue of the STATESMAN will be found an account of the manner in which Gen. Isaac I. Stevens—an honored citizen of this Territory, and repeatedly a recipient of the suffrages of its people—met his death. The first report in regard to his fate has been confirmed, to the lasting regret of the entire community. To add to the magnitude of the calamity, it occurred just at the time when his talents were being appreciated, and the highest military employments awaited him.

The singular mildness and placidity of Gen. Stevens' temper; his modesty and reserve among strangers, and the simplicity which marked his conduct when in high positions, have created a false impression as to his true character. His political connexions have been in a measure misunderstood, and his conduct misrepresented. Of one thing we are assured—*he has given his life for what he deemed a just cause*, and let those who would criticise him too closely at least show the same zeal for that cause or remain silent.

But it is only of Gen. Stevens' last days that we can speak without exciting differences of opinion, and they indeed afford an easy task for his eulogists...

...On the last day of his life the safety of the army depended on Stevens and Kearney, and they both put their lives in pawn and lost them. Who will say they did not do well? Although the loss is irreparable, they did do well. They left behind an example that is worth an army to those who survive. They have proven that the race of heroic men of the olden time is not yet extinct, and that amid the jealousies of commanders and the squabbles of factionists that there are those who see but the path of duty and dare to follow it to the grave. It was a time in which Generals again became soldiers and fought in person in the van; and here it was that Gen. Stevens proved himself no carpet-knight, but a man of mettle, who could look death in the face, and die...

...Among General Stevens' personal friends in this Territory his memory will be cherished and mingled with regrets at his untimely death; while there will be preserved a perpetual recollection of his untiring devotion to our interests—the great good which he has accomplished and the still greater benefits which, but for the present unfortunate civil strife, he intended to confer on the land of his adoption. While he is the last man with whom the people could willingly part, we can at least remember that he has been no unworthy champion of a great cause, but one who reflected honor upon it.

Death of Gen. I. I. Stevens.

A correspondent of the New York *Tribune*, in describing the battles which occurred near Fairfax and Centerville, on the first of September last, has the following relative to the death of Gen. Stevens, of Washington Territory, who fell in the battle of Chantilly:

WASHINGTON, Sept. 5.—The same hour that Gen. Stevens was killed in battle, a number of prominent gentlemen filling influential positions were in consultation in this city and in other parts of the country, with a view of having him assigned to the command of the army of Virginia. Successive manifestations of incapacity during a year of war have induced thinking men to cast about for a leader. These gentlemen had fixed upon Gen. Isaac I. Stevens as the man. His splendid conduct in the battles of Friday and Saturday had just attracted attention to him. It was remembered that in pure capacity he had always been first, having taken the honors at West Point with scarcely an effort, and though old political enemies, these men resolved to ask that he be given a leading command—while they were consulting he led on his men and fell...

...The army was retreating from Centerville. The battle was fought against a rebel force that had penetrated five miles nearer Washington than our rear, and was moving to strike upon the flank.— Gen. Stevens' division, the advance of Reno's corps, was on the left of the road taken by the trains, and intercepted the enemy. He saw that the rebels must be beaten back at once, or during the night they would stampede the wagons and probably so disconcert our retreat that the last divisions would fall a prey to their main force.— Decided to attack immediately, at the same time sending back for supplies. Having made positions, he led the attack on foot, at the head of the Seventy-ninth (Highlanders.) Soon a withering fire, and the Color Sergeant, Campbell, a grizzled old Scotchman, being hit, they faltered. One of the color guard seized the flag, when the General snatched it up. The wounded Highlander at his feet cried "God's sake, General, don't you take it, they'll shoot you if you do!" The General: "Give me the colors! If they don't I never will;" and he sprang forward. "We are all Highlanders; follow, follow, my Highlanders!" The Highlanders follow their Scottish chief, but toward a ball struck him on his temple, killed instantly. An hour afterward, his hands were clenched... on his staff.

DEATH OF ISAAC INGALLS STEVENS

Isaac Ingalls Stevens was appointed Washington Territory's first governor and then was elected the third territorial delegate to the U.S. Congress. Ambitious and energetic, he became the national campaign manager for the 1860 presidential ticket of John C. Breckenridge and Oregon's own Joseph Lane—the nominees of the southern wing of the Democratic Party. After Lincoln's election, Stevens worked hard to convene a national convention to work out sectional differences, hoping to amend the Constitution to protect slavery and thereby prevent secession and civil war. However, when war began in earnest, Stevens became convinced that his duty required defense of the United States against rebellion, and he joined the U.S. Army. Isaac Ingalls Stevens died on the battlefield at the Battle of Chantilly, in Virginia, on September 1, 1862. In this lithograph, we see Stevens in the uniform of a brigadier general in the U.S. Army. Additionally, here are excerpts from an article and an editorial in the *Walla Walla Statesman*, a Democratic newspaper in the territory that had been critical of Stevens's choice.

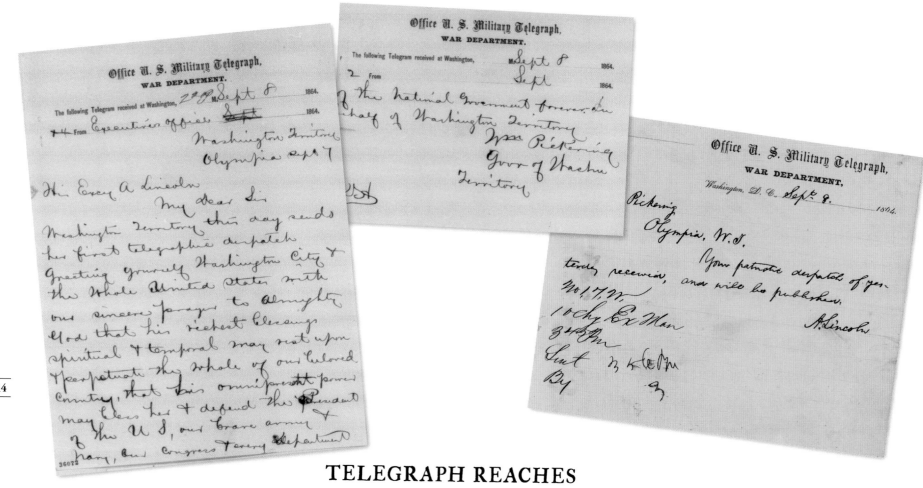

TELEGRAPH REACHES WASHINGTON TERRITORY!

When Abraham Lincoln entered the White House, his administration swept away Democratic patronage in Washington Territory, replacing Pierce and Buchanan Democrats with Lincoln Republicans. British-born William Pickering had served in the Illinois House of Representatives, considered Lincoln both a personal friend and a political colleague—Pickering led the Illinois delegation to the 1860 Republican National Convention, firmly committed to Lincoln, and then worked hard for his election. Once in office, President Lincoln rewarded Pickering with the choice of appointment as U.S. minister to England or the governorship of Washington Territory. Pickering chose the governorship and in June 1862 arrived in Olympia, where he served as the territory's wartime governor for more than four years. The telegraph finally arrived in Washington in September 1864; it was met with jubilation as the poles and the slender wire traveled north through the territory. On September 8, from Olympia, Governor Pickering sent a fulsome telegram to President Lincoln, transcribed at the War Office, in Washington, DC. The president was a busy man: Confederate troops had just surrendered Atlanta, and Lincoln was running for his second term. Lincoln's note for the reply to be telegraphed back to Pickering was hasty and terse, but written in his own hand.

Seattle, in 1873, from First Avenue South and Washington Street. Among prominent buildings shown are Masonic Hall, tower of M E Church, Wyckoff dwelling, the Pinkham, Naher, Sullivan, Meydenbauer, Robbins and Freeman stores; also Grose's barber shop, etc. The woods or tree line was Fifth Avenue, to Sixth.

Photographs by

REMEMBERING SEATTLE, 1873

Here you see a page from one of Thomas Prosch's albums of historic Seattle photographs. This one shows Seattle in 1873, looking north from the intersection of First Avenue and Washington Street. Prosch assembled these albums over a quarter century, annotating them with the rich information we see here in his handwriting. For instance, Prosch points out that the tree line in 1873, visible in the photograph, ran between Fifth and Sixth Avenues. Among the "prominent buildings" in the photograph, Prosch mentions Meydenbauer's "store" and Grose's barber shop. William and Sarah Grose (or Gross) were one of Seattle's first black families. Three years after Prosch's photograph was taken, Grose opened his Our House restaurant at the foot of Henry Yesler's wharf, a venture that would make Grose a very wealthy man and allow him to purchase the land that would become Seattle's Central District from Yesler. By 1873 William Meydenbauer had already earned a great deal of money in his little Eureka Bakery in Seattle, and had also staked his claim east across Lake Washington, on the Bellevue bay that bears his name. Prosch's album page shows us Seattle as a tiny boom-and-bust port town of false fronts and dirt streets, reeling from the dreadful news that the Northern Pacific Railroad had chosen Tacoma as the West Coast terminus of its transcontinental railroad.

15

SAMUEL GREENE VISITS SEATTLE

In these pages of Samuel Greene's reminiscence "A Sketch of My Life," he described a visit to Seattle that was nearly contemporary to the 1873 photograph shown in Prosch's album. Greene was a traveling minister, and keenly observant. Based on his journal, the "Sketch" is a treasure trove of detailed information about Washington Territory. I can also assure the reader from personal experience that very few handwritten accounts of the period are as clear and legible as Samuel Greene's. Leaving the steamer at Yesler's wharf, Greene walked up Yesler Way or Mill Street past the mill itself. Henry Yesler's sawmill had been running nearly continuously since March of 1853, sawing timber into lumber to be shipped throughout the Pacific. Among the wooden frame buildings, Greene noted Schwabacher's warehouse and general store, which was Seattle's first building made of brick, as well as Dexter Horton's bank, built of stone. Samuel Greene clearly perceived Seattle as a primitive place, from its rich crop of fleas to the stumps in the streets.

We found the city of Seattle containing about 800 people. Our boat landed at the wharf which was at the foot of Yesler Way — then known as Mill Street. At the extreme end of the dock was a warehouse, perhaps fifty feet wide by one hundred feet long. This was the only dock on the water-front, or at any point around Elliot Bay. This wharf was a very primitive affair. Landings were made with a gang plank wide enough to carry trucks side by side, with a lighter plank to be used by the passengers; though oftentimes when the tide was low the passengers must needs climb a ladder to the wharf floor.

Returning now to Seattle: As the arrival walked up the wharf he would note the Yesler sawmill on his left hand; and proceeding up Mill Street (Yesler Way) he found the roadway paved with sawdust. Just before this was the Occidental Hotel. On his right was Commercial Street, and on his left Front Street, so-called. These two streets did not coincide as First Avenue and First Avenue, South now do.

At the corner of Commercial St., and on southward were plain, simple frame buildings with the single-story brick building known as Swabacher.

About three or four doors south from Mill Street, on the corner of Front and Mill streets, about where the south east corner of the little park on Pioneer Square now is, was a neat shop in a wooden frame building; while north of that were other wooden buildings ... for a block or two. In this vicinity were all of the eight or ten business stores and offices of the city; although the Dexter Horton private bank, a small rough stone building northwest corner of Main and commercial streets, while on the southeast of Front and Cherry was Yesler ... or the Pavilion, as it was sometimes ...

It was interesting to the occasional arrivals from the South, as they walked to the Occidental Hotel — oftentimes in the summer dressed in their white suits — to find the fleas from the sawdust nearly covering the lower parts of their clothing. I think everybody declared that they never were in a region where there were as many fleas as were found hereabouts. There was certainly no place where a flea could jump quicker and farther: they were the athletes of the community at that time.

There was not a single block of streets that had been opened or graded. The stumps could be seen in what is now First Avenue, as far south as Cherry St., and the wagon tracks wound round among them. A new vehicle of any kind was seldom seen: Mr. A. A. Denny had the only covered conveyance to be found in the city, and that was a small single-seated buggy.

In the matter of the Estate

Carrie E. Clark, Deceased.

Inventory and appraisement.

Personal Estate	
Cooking Stove & fixtures	5 00
4 and irons	1 00
1 8 day clock	3 00
Kitchen furniture tin war Crockery &c.	5 00
One flour & meal box with fixtures	1 50
„ Spring balance	38
1 Turpentine lantern	75
2 Kitchen tables	1 75
1 assorted fruit	2 00
1 Stone jug	1 25
1 Can lard 10 lb.	1 25
1 cloths wringer	3 00
1 Lot carpenters tools	10 00
1 Bottles jars & cans	2 00
1 Beadstead Mattrass & wash Stand	8 00
1 Lot of Books & pictures	5 00
1 Sewing Machine	10 00
1 Table	1 50
1 Pressey bedroom set.	10 00
1 Mattrass & two beds	5 00
4 Pillows @ 50	2 00
1 Lot of chickens	1 50
1 Black Walnut table	5 00
1 Map W.T.	25
1 Parlor stove with zinc	5 00
1 Lot Stove pipe	50
1 Looking glass	1 00
Carpeting for 2 rooms oil cloth	20 00

A PROBATED ESTATE

Public records are rich sources of information about the ordinary people who lived everyday lives in the past. Here we see an 1874 case file from the probate records of the Thurston County clerk. Carrie E. Clark died intestate—without a will—and this inventory of her personal estate was likely conducted prior to a public auction, held to satisfy her creditors. Without researching Clark further in the territorial census or other records, this provocative document raises as many questions as it provides answers. Was Clark young or old? A spinster? A widow? Did she have any heirs? Why are there two bedsteads listed, if she lived alone? Did she use the carpenter's tools? Or the sewing machine? Did she make her living as a seamstress? There are some special personal items—the looking glass, the map of Washington Territory, the books and pictures— what do they suggest about Carrie E. Clark and the way she lived and died?

POOR FARM LEDGER, SEATTLE

In March 1877 Reverend Emil Kauten, assistant pastor of Our Lady of Good Help Catholic Church in Seattle, invited Mother Praxedes, superior of the Sisters of Providence, at Vancouver, Washington Territory, to help establish the King County Poor Farm. The Sisters of Providence agreed to care for the poor at the cost of seventy-five cents per person, per day. Here you see the first page of their first patient ledger, May 1877 into September 1878. Archival research yields many lists, but this one is extraordinary for the evidence it provides about indigence in territorial Seattle. Seattle's poor came from all over the world, although no Asian can be found on this list. Most were male; most had "professions," ranging from sea captain to miner, and many were simple "labourers." Some poor folks were very ill when they came into the Sisters' care, and fully one-third of them died during this period.

PROVIDENCE HOSPITAL, SEATTLE, WASHINGTON.

No.	Name.	Country.	Age.	Sex. M.	Sex. F.	Residence.	Religion.	Profession.	Entered. Year.	Month.	Day.	Discharged. Year.	Month.	Day.	Died. Year.	Month.	Day.	Remarks.
1	John Benson	Norway	43	1		White River W. T.	Non Catho	Labourer	1877	May	19							
2	Alexander Barret	Canada	35	2		Seattle " "	caths	"	"	"	24	1877			1877	July	12	
3	Mary Tucker	Mullato	19		1	" " "	2		"	"	26	"			"	Oct.	28	
4	John Tucker	"	2 Month	3		" " "	3		"	"	"	"	June	16				
5	Willie Larkman	Half Breed	18	4		Swinomish " "	2	Labourer	"	June	3	"	"					
6	Frank Nossankoski	Strasburgh	26	5		Seattle " "	3	4	"	"	"	"	"		1878	Oct.	1	
7	Samuel Fox	Poland	51	6		Seattle	5	Gas Worker	"	"	5	"	"	14				
8	Thomas Schafer	America	36	7		Slaughter (White River)	6	Farmer	"	"	10	"	Aug.	30				
9	William Williams	Germany	46	8		Seattle W. T.	7	Labourer	"	"	11	"			1877	June	14	
10	Robert Turnbull	America	54	9		" " "	8	"	"	"	20	"			"	Oct.	14	
11	Charles Munroe		34	10		" " "	4		"	Aug.	2	1878	June	11				
12	Terence O'Brien	Ireland	60	11		White River " "	5	Farmer	"	"	4	1877	Dec.	13				
13	Alex. Barren	America	60	12		Seattle " "	9	Labourer	"	"	14	"	Aug.	8				
14	James Cronan	Ireland	39	13		" " "	6	"	"	"	16	"	"	21				
15	Charles A. Collins	America	27	14		" " "	10	"	"	"	22	1878	Apl.	7				
16	Pat. Harrigan	Ireland	43	15		White River " "	7	"	"	"	27	"			"	Aug.	24	
17	Mrs. James Regan	"	34		2	Seattle " "	8		"	Sept.	20	1877	Oct.	16				
18	Henry Amby	Coloured Man	54	16		" " "	11	Cook	"	Oct.	3	"	Sept.	26				
19	Joseph Lynch	Ireland	15	17		" " "	9	Student	"	"	12	"			"	Nov.	16	
20	Alvin Chapin	America	38	18		" " "	12	Mechanic	"	"	15	"	Oct.	28				
21	James Coy		44	19		" " "	10	Engineer	"	"	16	"			"	Oct.	31	
22	William Frechette	Canada	38	20		" " "	11	Cook	"	"	20	"			"	"	19	
23	Chris. Newman	German	43	21			13	Labourer	"	Nov.	13	1878	Apl.	19				
24	John Sullivan	Ireland	22	22			12		"	Dec.	4	"			1878	Apl.	19	
25	H. L. Gilbert	Fort Rangle Alaska	49	23			14	Miner	"	"	19	1877	Dec.	13				
26	James Hicks	England	51	24		Free Port " "	15	Labour	1878	Feb.	11	1878	Feb.	6				
27	James Kelly	Ireland	25	25		Seattle " "	16	Fireman	"	Mar.	16	"	June	2				
28	Manuel Polepasual	Chili	35	26		" " "	17	Fisherman	"	April	17	"	Sept.	21				
29	Pat. Clancy	Ireland	25	27		" " "	13	Miner	"	"	26	"	Dec.	3				
30	Alfred Wilson	Sweden	36	28		" " "	18	Labourer	"	May	30	"	June	12				
31	Anthony Haron	Ireland	57	29		White River " "	14	Farmer		June	4	"	Sept.	11				
32	Lewis Sperry	America	71	30		Seattle " "	19	Netter	"	"	10	"			"	June	26	
33	John O'Brien	"	19	31		White River " "	15	20	Farmer	"	"	24	"	June	18				
34	Charles Drew	Canada	42	32		Seattle " "	21	Engineer	"	"	29	"	"	29				
35	Louis Lacraty		35	33		Whatcom " "	16	Labourer	"	July	4	"			"	July	2	
36	Antonio Bodnich	Austria	30	34		Seattle " "	14	Fisherman	"	Aug.	1	"			"	"	25	
37	John Macken	Ireland	37	35		" " "	20	Labourer	"	"	8	"	Aug.	23				
38	Thomas Morrison	America	36	36		" " "	21	"	"	"	15	"			1878	Mar.	6	
39		"		37		" " "	22	Smith	"	"	17				1878	Aug.	24	
										Sept.	4							

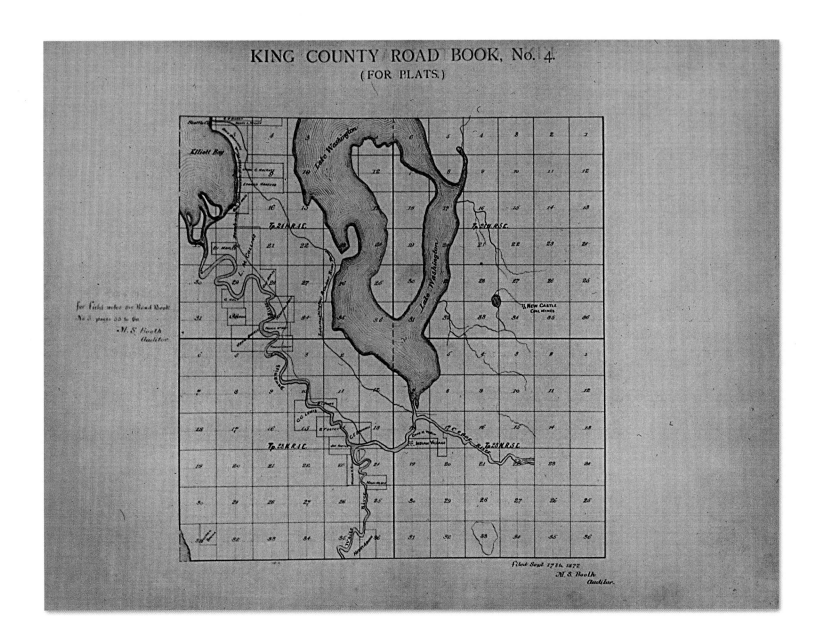

KING COUNTY ROAD BOOK, No. 4.
(FOR PLATS.)

ROAD SURVEY, KING COUNTY

This map shows the Duwamish River and the area to the east in August 1877, and reflects King County's original platting, as well as the Beach and Duwamish River Road and the Lake Washington and Cedar River Road. Drawn in King County Road Book 4, the map clearly shows Seattle's tideflats, the meandering Duwamish River, and Lake Washington and some of its islands and rivers, long before civil engineering changed those places and waterways forever. Land claims are clearly identified on the document and include many familiar Seattle names, from Maynard and Yesler to van Asselt and Holgate, as well as the Newcastle coal mines and the "Indian Village" near present-day Renton.

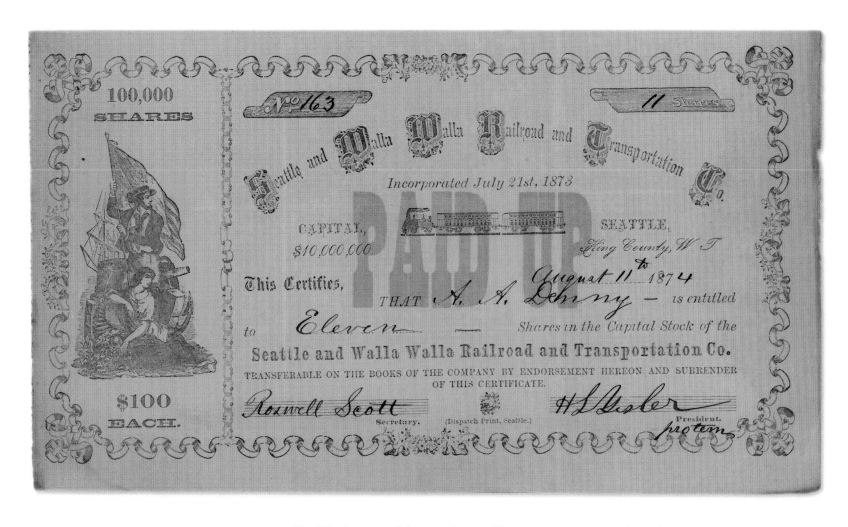

INVESTING IN SEATTLE'S OWN RAILROAD

The Northern Pacific's 1873 choice of Tacoma as the railroad's West Coast terminus seemed to seal Seattle's fate to forever be one of a dozen second-class small ports on Puget Sound. But the town's business leaders rallied behind a daring notion—to build their own railroad. The Seattle and Walla Walla Railroad was incorporated in July 1873 to construct a narrow gauge line from Seattle's waterfront all the way to Walla Walla, where it would intersect with the Northern Pacific Railroad. Arthur Armstrong Denny had traveled the Oregon Trail with his family, arriving at Alki Point in West Seattle in November 1851 and relocating to the eastern shore of Elliott Bay the following spring. He brought a dream to the West: that there would soon be a transcontinental railroad across the northern states and territories that would terminate on Puget Sound; he hoped his fortunes would grow with the country once it was accessible by rail. Faced with the Northern Pacific's decision, Denny became president of the Seattle and Walla Walla Railroad. Here we see a stock certificate from 1878 for eleven shares of stock. The Seattle and Walla Walla Railroad slowly advanced southeast and opened the coal mines of Renton and Newcastle, bringing coal by rail directly to the bunkers on Elliott Bay. But the railroad never did reach Walla Walla.

SOME WESTERN WASHINGTON TOWNS, 1882–1883

City directories offer wonderful opportunities to researchers. Strictly speaking, such volumes are not archival since they have been published. However, older directories, like this *Disturnell's Business Directory* from 1882–3, are so rare and their evidence is so terrific, it seems doctrinaire to ignore them. Here we see pages 540 and 541 from this directory held in the Seattle Public Library's Seattle Collection. *Disturnell's* only lists business owners and is not particularly useful for genealogical researchers, but these thumbnail descriptions of Washington Territory's towns in the 1880s will delight family and local historians. How wonderful to learn of the rousing cattle industry at Oysterville, where tanneries and oyster beds existed side by side. Or the thriving sawmill and shipyard at Port Blakely, and the huge sawmill at Port Gamble. Or the "beautiful and charming" site of Port Townsend, whose "air of prosperity" and "basis of permanence and solidity . . . augur[ed] well for its future," despite the then-current economic slump.

"THE CHINESE MUST GO."

A Large Delegation from All Points on the Sound Assemble in Yesler's Hall this Afternoon and Take Preliminary Action Against the Heathen Horde.

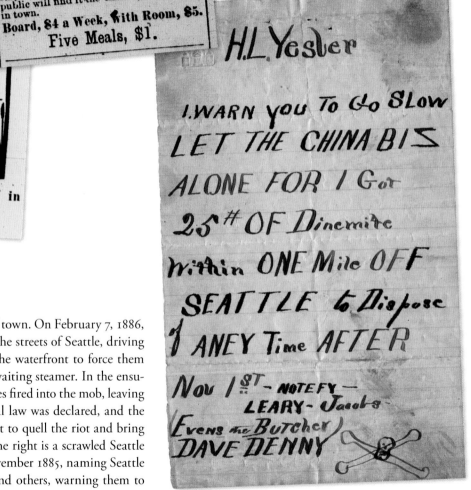

The Chinese Must Go!

THE SEATTLE RESTAURANT!

UNDER NEW MANAGEMENT.

A. J. TICE has purchased the Seattle Restaurant and employs nothing but white help. Traveling public will find it the BEST and CHEAPEST in town.

Board, $4 a Week, with Room, $5.

Five Meals, $1.

H.L Yesler

I. WARN YOU TO GO SLOW
LET THE CHINA BIS
ALONE FOR I GOT
25 # OF Dinemite
Within ONE MILE OFF
SEATTLE to Dispose
I ANEY Time AFTER
Nov 1ST — NOTEFY —
LEARY- Jacobs
Evens the Butcher
DAVE DENNY

ANTI-CHINESE HATE CRIME

Led by the Knights of Labor, resentment of Chinese workers grew along the West Coast, cresting in fall and winter 1885–86. This agitation targeted Chinese men who were willing to work harder, longer, and for lower wages than white men. The masthead block of the *Seattle Daily Call* was published with slight variations in city newspapers in California, Oregon, and Washington. However, anti-Chinese hate crimes also took place in the countryside. On the night of September 7, 1885, shots were fired into a group of Chinese hops pickers asleep in their tents in Issaquah, and three died. Agitation against the Chinese increased in the Puget Sound region, as shown by the Seattle Restaurant's advertisement in the *Daily Call* (September 21, 1885). In Tacoma, in November of 1885, carefully organized squads evicted Chinese workers, driving nearly 600 men to trains headed out of town. On February 7, 1886, a mob raced through the streets of Seattle, driving the city's Chinese to the waterfront to force them to leave the city on a waiting steamer. In the ensuing riot, Seattle deputies fired into the mob, leaving one man dead. Martial law was declared, and the state militia turned out to quell the riot and bring order to the city. To the right is a scrawled Seattle bomb threat from November 1885, naming Seattle mayor Henry Yesler and others, warning them to leave the "China biz" alone—in other words, to not interfere in plans to drive Chinese workers away. Also here is a list of the Chinese businesses burned to the ground by arsonists in Tacoma. On March 9, 1886, the Seattle *Daily Call* published the poem "Quietly Leaving," excerpted here.

near the Wharf

New Tacoma W.T.

的欽巴埠被逐焚燒各鋪名冊列壬票

北真隆伙食店舖 郭非芷捉 貨物盡被焚燒
Shue King Lung Store
廣昌昌伙食舖 沅年芷捉 貨物盡被焚燒
Quong Mou Chong Store
昌隆伙食舖 沅忠芷捉 貨物盡被變燒
Chong Lung Store
履信伙食舖 沅三芷捉 貨物盡被焚燒
Luck Sun Store
裕昌隆疋菜舖 湯順芷捉 貨物盡被焚燒
Yee Chong Vegetable Store
占記昌洗承館 翁扶芷捉 什物盡被焚燒
Jun Lee Chong Laundry
鵬利堂洗毛住者 物件盡被焚燒
Sing Lee Family
廣森�別館舖 沅裕仁芷捉 貨物盡被焚燒
Quong Wo Tai Butch Shop
沅南榮住者 什物盡被焚燒
Yuen Mone Family
廣祥源伙食舖 住廣華芷捉 貨物盡被焚燒
Quong Chong Yuen Store

Life in Town

的欽埠山頂被逐連失貨物銀兩各鋪名冊列壬票

三興伙食舖 林型芷捉 貨物銀兩盡被逐失
Sun Hing Store
廿日利伙食舖 伍意獨芷捉 貨物銀兩盡被逐失
Yee Lee Store
美華洗承館 陳錄搭芷捉 物件銀兩盡被逐失
Mee Wah Laundry
捷利洗承館 洪祥謹芷捉 物件銀兩盡被逐失
Seuck Lee Laundry
占記洗承館 伍如三芷捉 物件銀兩盡被逐失
Jun Lee Laundry
同利洗承館 陳宗語芷捉 物件銀兩盡被逐失
Kong Lee Laundry
廣興禾菜舖 林政查芷捉 的貨銀兩盡被逐失
Quong Hing Vegetable Store
新昌伙食舖 吳變九對捉 貨物銀兩盡被逐失
Sun Chong Store
榮利洗承館 陳家住芷捉 物件銀兩盡被逐失
Wing Lee Laundry
捷記洗承館 陳炳國芷捉 物件銀兩盡被逐失

MARCH 6, 1886.　　HARPER'S WEEKLY.　　157

THE ANTI-CHINESE RIOT AT SEATTLE, WASHINGTON TERRITORY.—DRAWN BY W. P. SNYDER, FROM SKETCHES BY J. F. WHITING, OF SEATTLE.—[SEE PAGE 155.]
1. Driving Chinamen on Board of the Steamer.　2. Marching under Guard to the Court-house.

Quietly Leaving.

The greatest advertisement that Seattle yet has seen
Was the leaving of the Chinese on the famous steamship Queen.
All people turned out in a mass to see the lepers go.
Well, did they leave? "Not all of them." There's some still here, you know.
You see there's some folks in our town that have no heart or soul;
They'll harbor the hated Chinese and cause the funeral bells to toll.
Great God! is not one life enough to fill their hearts with pain?
No! They still hire Chinamen to bring this on again.
Any loyal citizen will stop to reason once
And say, "John Chinaman, you go, I'll not be called a dunce."
They'll thus regain lost friendship, and all this trouble end;
And every starving white will say, "There's another white man's friend."
Some give their clothes to Chinamen to take away and wash
And say "they can't do otherwise;" but that is simply "bosh."
There's white laundries here to do their work; they could get them if they would.
But then you see white people would reap the benefit if they should.

23

PUGET SOUND BUSINESSES, 1887

The *Puget Sound Directory* of 1887 is filled with the ambition of the towns on the Sound. Reading the advertisements on these pages, you can sense the eager opportunism caused by the Northern Pacific's completion and the anticipation of statehood. Tacoma's full-page ad eagerly trumpeted its destiny: to become the great hub of rail and steamship transportation on Puget Sound, inviting investors and homebuyers to purchase lots in the city. The Switchback Saloon in Tacoma also referenced the Northern Pacific's terminus and offered the best Kentucky bourbon, San Francisco lager beer, and domestic cigars in the area. On the other hand, La Conner's McGlinn House catered to abstainers by selling no liquor and promising the joys of a quiet stay and a large reading room. In Port Townsend the Hong Yung Restaurant and Chinese Employment Service provided "neat, careful laborers" for local work—just one year after the anti-Chinese riots. And in Seattle, heavy industry brought jobs and built a base of skilled metalworkers, while Smith's Bijou Theatre advertised the largest and best entertainment in the Northwest, proud of five years of "phenomenal success."

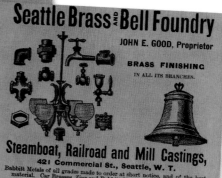

WALLA WALLA CENSUS PAGE

In 1887 most people were confident that Washington Territory would soon achieve statehood, and its citizens would finally have the opportunity to elect the governor, to send voting representatives to the U.S. Senate and House of Representatives, and to cast their ballots in presidential races. The federal census was held throughout the United States every ten years, beginning in 1790. However, the 1890 census for Washington State—as for many other states—was destroyed by fire, and the territorial censuses for 1887 and 1889 consequently take on particular significance for researchers. This page of the 1887 Walla Walla County census allows us to follow the census taker as he walked or rode his horse from place to place, enumerating residents as he came across them. We can see that no black men or women were counted in this part of Walla Walla County, but that three young Chinese men lived there. The large age difference between some men and their wives is striking, as are the single-parent families. The clusters of single women and single men suggest vocational groups or boarding-houses—perhaps a few men working at a mining operation and a few women working as cooks and waitresses. And one wonders, of course, how many children were eventually born to the productive Painter family . . .

NEVADA BLOOMER

Washington women had been granted the right to vote in 1883 by the territorial legislature, but the statute was struck down three years later by the territorial supreme court. Amid tremendous public controversy, the territorial legislature enacted new legislation in January 1888 that clearly stated that all residents of the state, male or female, were entitled to vote. Four months later, the wonderfully named Mrs. Nevada Bloomer was refused the right to cast her ballot and brought suit against the election officials in Spokane Falls. However, Nevada Bloomer was actually backed by the liquor industry and had an ulterior motive—to force the issue back to court and invalidate the suffrage legislation. Women had consistently voted in Washington Territory to further moral reform, supporting what today we would call "family values." The supreme court of Washington Territory held that the 1888 Suffrage Bill had violated federal law, arguing, "[T]he word 'citizen' was used [by the framers of the Constitution] as a qualification for voting and holding office, and, in our judgment, the word then meant and still signifies male citizenship, and must so be construed." Washington women were barred from the franchise until 1910. The summons shown here was issued to the election officials in the case.

STATEHOOD!
FINALLY!

In February 1889, the U.S. Congress sent legislation to President Grover Cleveland, for his signature. The Omnibus Bill, as it was called, set the course for the territories of Washington, North Dakota, South Dakota, and Montana to qualify for statehood. Delegates from throughout Washington met during the summer of 1889 to hammer out a state constitution, which would be submitted to the voters for approval. They also asked the voters whether women should be given the franchise, where the state capital should be, and whether liquor should be prohibited in the new state. The voters approved retaining the capital at Olympia, and voted against prohibition and votes for women. And they approved the new constitution by 40,152 to 11,789 votes. Finally, after thirty-six years of waiting and at least two failed attempts at statehood, Washington Territory became a state on November 11, 1889. The transcribed telegram below was sent by Secretary of State James G. Blaine to Governor Elisha Ferry, the first governor of the brand-new state. President Benjamin Harrison had signed the proclamation admitting Washington Territory as a state, to tremendous rejoicing in the Northwest.

Form No. 1.

THE WESTERN UNION TELEGRAPH COMPANY.

This Company TRANSMITS and DELIVERS messages only on conditions limiting its liability, which have been assented to by the sender of the following message. Errors can be guarded against only by repeating a message back to the sending station for comparison, and the company will not hold itself liable for errors or delays in transmission or delivery of Unrepeated Messages, beyond the amount of tolls paid thereon, nor in any case where the claim is not presented in writing within sixty days after sending the message.
This is an UNREPEATED MESSAGE, and is delivered by request of the sender, under the conditions named above.

THOS. T. ECKERT, General Manager.   NORVIN GREEN, President.

NUMBER | SENT BY | REC'D BY | 29 Collect—61c | CHECK | Via Olympia

Received at Olympia   Nov 11 1889

Dated Olympia Executive Mansion Washington 11

To Gov Elisha P. Ferry

The president signed the proclamation declaring Washington to be a state in the union at five oclock and twenty seven minutes this afternoon

Jas G Blaine

THREE GREAT FIRES

Three devastating fires swept the cities of Washington Territory during the statehood summer. On June 7, 1889, thirty-two blocks of Seattle—the city's entire business and commercial district—burned to the ground. On the night of July 4, a fire began in a grocery store that consumed the town of "Ellensburgh," as the *Seattle Times* reporter spelled it. And on August 5, forty blocks of Spokane—again, the city's heart—were also consumed by flames. In all three cases, 1889's particularly hot, dry summer combined with strong winds was largely to blame. A spark was all that was needed. Low water levels hindered the efforts of volunteer firemen to douse the flames.

Newspaper accounts make clear that these dense cities of wooden buildings, dry as tinder in the summer heat, burned so fiercely that the urban fires did not stop until they ran out of fuel. In the boom decade of the 1880s, Seattle, Ellensburg, and Spokane had grown too fast, without good building codes, professional fire departments, or adequate fire-fighting equipment. Two men died during the Spokane fire but generally, there was little loss of life though great loss of property. However, these three city sites were swept clean by their fires for construction of new cities that were better designed, with more modern infrastructure.

DAN BOONE
AND FAMILY

Which families had deep roots in this place, and which families arrived in Washington by wagon, train, or ship? Photos of a very few of them are scattered through this book of documentary history. Here we see Dan Boone and his family in about 1900. Boone was Native American and worked as the saddle and harness maker at Fort Simcoe, near Yakima. This photo shows how his family both assimilated into the new culture and retained their own traditional culture.

Rules and Regulations

For the Government of Schools and Teachers, adopted by the Board of Education.

A TEACHER'S DUTY.

TO THE SCHOOL AUTHORITIES.

1. To understand and enforce the rules and regulations of the Board of eduction.

2. To carry out faithfully the instructions of the Superintendent and the principal of the school.

3. To keep your school records, use your school blanks, and render your school reports exactly according to instructions.

TO SCHOOL PROPERTY.

4. To make your school-room a pleasant and attractive place for children; ornamenting it, when possible, with pictures.

5. To take good care of all the books, maps, charts, blanks, keys, and other school property entrusted to your care.

6. To inspect daily the stoves, desks, and other school property, and instantly report to the principal or teacher whenever any damage is done.

TO PUPILS.

7. To know that the best school teaching is always associated with the best school government, and that good school government consists in having each pupil attend quietly and faithfully to *his own* business, at his own desk, which is his place of business.

8. To know that a pupil's true education is a *growth* consequent upon the proper exercise of his faculties.

9. To make yourself acquainted with the home influences affecting your pupils.

10. To make yourself acquainted with the moral, intellectual, and physical natures of your pupils, and to teach every one according to his nature.

11. To inspire your pupils with *enthusiasm* in the pursuit of knowledge, and to implant in them *aspirations* for all attainable excellence.

12. To keep your pupils *busy* with school work, and to work your classes upon the prescibed course of study.

13. To attend to the proper position of pupils, when sitting, standing, or moving in the school-room.

14. To teach your pupils *how* to study.

15. To *talk* in a natural tone of voice.

16. To commend pupils for earnest work.

17. To teach the virtues of industry, order, system, promptness, punctuality and attention to business, and the value of time and its improvement.

18. To teach the ways of getting knowledge, and the reasons for and value of good school order.

19. To remember that children *are* children, and need assistance in many ways, but that the most valuable work for a pupil is that which he does for himself.

20. To know that mistakes, blunders, neglect, or carelessness on your part, are disastrous to pupils, and are most difficult to remedy.

21. To be ever thoughtful of the pupil's future, and to make all school work and discipline such as will be of lasting service to them.

22. To keep pupils *happy*, and to remember that what a pupil *grows to be* is of more importance than what he *lives to know*.

TO YOURSELF.

23. To use every effort to improve yourself in the science and art of governing and teaching a school.

24. To exercise a watchful care over every word and act; teaching by example as well as by precept.

25. To be systematic and methodical in all your work.

26. To keep such private record of your own work that at any time you may be able to give the important facts in connection with any year of your school service.

27. To be very cautious, careful, and circumspect in everything you say and do in the presence of your pupils.

TO THE SCHOOL.

28. To have a carefully prepared programme for daily exercises, and to follow it closely in your work.

29. To *talk* little, and in a natural tone of voice, but *do* much in school.

30. To rely upon your own tact, skill, energy, and devotion to your work.

31. To be at your post in time, or never to be tardy.

32. To give your undivided attention to school duties, never reading books, making out school reports, nor writing letters during school hours.

33. To keep neat files of all reports, records, circulars, letters, and business papers.

34. To speak the English language in its purity.

35. To feel an honest pride in your school, and a determination to have it take high rank among schools.

TO PARENTS.

36. To avoid wounding the feelings of any parent by word or manner.

37. To endeavor to secure the confidence and co-operation of parents in your efforts to benefit their children.

38. To know that a dispassionate conversation with a parent will almost invariably convince him that you are pursuing a correct course with his child.

39. To keep parents fully informed of the doings and progress of their children.

TO OTHER TEACHERS.

40. To aid and encourage fellow-teachers by a a friendly appreciation of their work and efforts.

A PUPIL'S DUTY.

TO THE SCHOOL.

1. To observe and obey the rules and regulations of the school.

2. To be prompt and regular in attendance at school.

3. To do your full part in making your school the best possible.

IN THE SCHOOL HOUSE.

4. To attend quietly and faithfully to *your own business*, at your own desk, during school hours.

5. To avoid disturbing teachers and school-mates by unnecessary noise, such as dropping books or pencils, or moving feet upon the floor in changing position.

6. To avoid wasting your time, or that of your school-mates, by whispering or otherwise taking their attention from their school duties.

7. To recite lessons promptly, and in a full, natural tone of voice, pronouncing every word very distinctly.

8. To do all slate, chart, paper, and black-board work with the greatest rapidity consistent with neatness and accuracy.

OUTSIDE THE SCHOOL HOUSE.

9. To go to and from school in such a manner as not to disturb any one.

10. To go home directly at the close of school, and not come to the school-house before the proper time.

11. To move quietly about the school-house and make no unnecessary noise in its neighborhood.

TO TEACHERS.

12. To be obedient and respectful to parents and teachers.

13. To render teachers proper excuses for any absence or tardiness.

14. To obey promptly and cheerfully all signals of teachers.

TO PROPERTY.

15. Never to cut, mar, mark, or injure desks, walls, fences, or any school property whatever.

16. To keep books and slates covered, to keep your school-desk and its contents in good order, and the floor about your desk neat and clean.

TO YOURSELF.

17. To be always neat and tidy in dress and person.

18. To do the very best you can in all school or other work you may have to do.

19. To be mindful of the rights and feelings of others, and to be kind and polite to all.

GENERAL DUTIES.

20. To remember that energy and patient industry, enthusiasm and earnestness, are the surest reliance for success in student-life as well as in business or professional life.

21. To remember that there is a time for work, for play, and for study, and that the school-room is the place for study.

22. To feel and understand the great value of time, and learn ways of improving it.

23. To let no day pass without adding something to your store of knowledge.

24. To be truthful, and use *good language* on all occasions.

DUTIES OF TEACHERS AND STUDENTS

The Washington State Board of Education's 1891 annual report included this list of the mutual duties and responsibilities of teacher and student. These rules and regulations offer an intriguing perspective on the expectations of education in the state's one-room schoolhouses and city classrooms, just after statehood. Teachers were encouraged to teach each child "according to his nature," and expected to model the values and virtues of a life committed to teaching. Students were encouraged to see school as a preparation for life, and to practice the lifelong virtues of "energy and patient industry, enthusiasm and earnestness."

HOPS FARM TIME BOOK

Lars Wold and his brothers Peter and Ingebright emigrated from Norway in the 1860s; they were among the first settlers to make land claims in the Issaquah area. In 1868 the brothers purchased hops starts from Puyallup settler Ezra Meeker, to grow the indispensable, lucrative ingredient in brewing beer. The Wolds employed Chinese workers in the 1880s, and it was on their farm that three Chinese were shot to death in their tents as they slept. During the 1890s, regional hops farms were plagued by the hop louse, as it was called, that destroyed the crop. Many farmers gave up on their hops and replaced them with an easier crop, but Lars Wold was stubborn and held out until 1901, when he turned his hops farm into a dairy. Here we see a page from Wold's carefully kept time book that recorded who picked how much for what wage, at a time when most of his workers were local Native men and women.

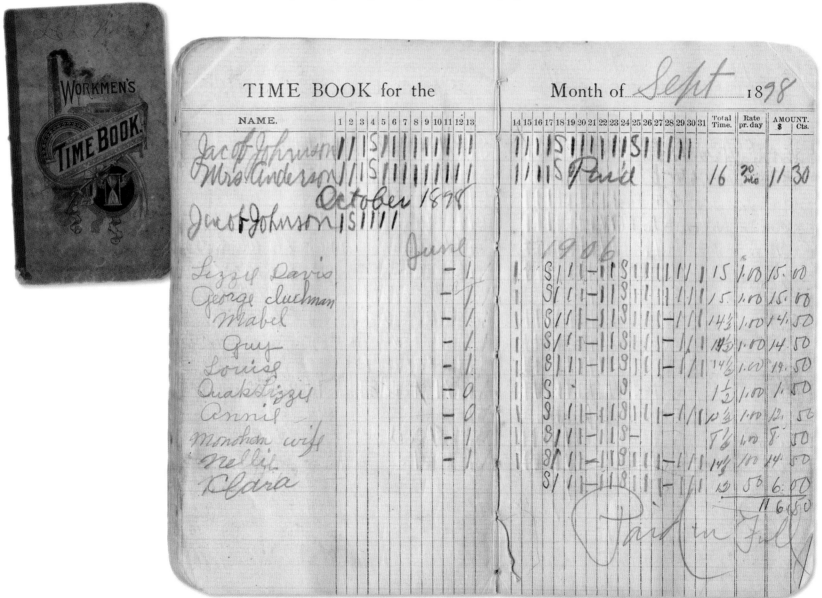

Topeka Kansas,
Feb. 16. 1897.

Gov. J. R. Rogers,
  Olympia Washington.

        Dear Sir— Enclosed is partial copy of introductory letter given me by Mr. Clark, Chairman State Central Com. Peoples Party, Denver Colorado,— My home.—

        Early next April, a party of six, including myself intend to start for Washington with a view of locating a colony of about one hundred, honest, industrious, intelligent progressive people, the majority of them farmers from Kansas and Colorado; and all believers in free land, free water, free air and free sunshine.

        Any information You can give us will be highly appreciated; and if we settle in your State, we shall be glad to reciprocate any courtesies that you may be able to extend to us. — Sincerely Yours
                        Sidney A. Gaylor,
                        Topeka Kan.

5-26. Topeka ave.

POPULIST AGRARIAN COLONY

In the 1890s the U.S. economy struggled to find its way—one critic remarked that economic injustice had created two classes in America: millionaires and tramps. In 1892 the Populist Party organized in Omaha around the principles of direct democracy, urban labor's right to organize, and the farmers' right to fair prices. Specifically, the Populists advocated the right of recall, initiative, and referendum; direct election of senators (until 1913, they were elected by state legislators); a graduated income tax; the coinage of silver to expand the money supply; government ownership of the railroads; and other reforms that were seen as quite radical at the time. In Washington State, the 1880s boom had brought thousands of newcomers to the state, eager for jobs, but by 1896 Washington was struggling with unemployment that showed no signs of letting up. In Washington, "fusion" between state Democrats, Silver Republicans, and Populists provided majorities at the ballot box, electing Populist gubernatorial candidate John Rogers and providing him with Fusion majorities in both houses of the legislature. Rogers was widely known for his Populist writings, including *The Irrepressible Conflict; or An American System of Money*, 1892; *The Rights of Man and The Wrongs of Man*, 1893; *Politics: An Argument in Favor of the Inalienable Rights of Man*, 1894; *Homes for the Homeless*, 1895 and *Free Land: The Remedy for Involuntary Poverty*, 1897. Here we see a letter to Rogers from a fellow member of the People's Party, hoping to start a Washington State agrarian colony of "honest, industrious, intelligent progressive people . . . all believers in free land, free water, free air and free sunshine."

HO FOR THE KLONDIKE!

When the steamer *Portland* docked in Seattle on July 17, 1897, its passengers included sixty-eight ordinary men who among them carried nearly $2 million in gold dust and nuggets, panned along the streams of the Yukon River. The Klondike Gold Rush hit Seattle, struggling in a national depression, like a whirlwind. The city's mayor resigned his office to head for the Klondike, as did many newspaper reporters and policemen—there weren't enough ships to accommodate the demand to race to the goldfields. Then Seattle's movers and shakers realized that it was possible to make a killing by staying at home, mining the miners themselves. Seattle's Chamber of Commerce mounted an international campaign, touting the city at the terminus of the Great Northern Railway as the place for would-be miners to outfit themselves, have a good time, buy transportation to Skagway, and then have their gold dust assayed. Seattle grew rich on the Gold Rush, and this Cooper & Levy ad from the *Seattle Times*, August 23, 1897, shows one reason why. Each miner spent about $200 outfitting himself with these supplies, and between 1897 and 1910, about 100,000 miners pulsed through Seattle. The Klondike Gold Rush bankrolled Seattle's growth into the major city on Puget Sound.

KLONDIKE

Supplies for One Man for One Year

Flour .... 400 lbs	Knives and forks .... 1 each
Corn meal, 3-lbs .... 20 lbs	Spoons .... 3 tea and 3 table
Rolled oats, 4-lb .... 36 lbs	Spoons (basting) .... 1 large
Rice .... 25 lbs	Quaker bread pan 1
Beans .... 100 lbs	Cups, granite 2
Sugar .... 75 lbs	Plates, granite 3
Saccharin, powdered or tablets....	Whetstone 1
Dried fruits, apples, peaches,	Coffee pots 1
apricots, assorted .... 75 lbs	Sled 1
Dried raisins .... 10 lbs	Pick and handle 1
Yeast cakes (6 in pkg) .... 12 pkgs	Prospector's pick 1
Candles .... 1 box of 120	Hatchet 1
Dry salt pork .... 25 lbs	Saws, whip 1
Evaporated potatoes .... 25 lbs	Saws, hand 1
Evaporated onions .... 10 lbs	Shovels 1
Butter .... 20 lbs	Nails .... 20 lbs
Bacon .... 150 lbs	Files, assorted .... ½ doz
Dried beef .... 30 lbs	Ax and handle 1
Extract of beef (4 oz.) .... ½ doz	Draw knife 1
Baking powder .... 10 lbs	Plane 1
Soda .... 3 lbs	Brace and bit 1
Salt .... 20 lbs	Chisels, assorted 3
Pepper .... 1 lb	Butcher knife 1
Mustard .... ½ lb	Sheath knife 1
Ginger .... ¼ lb	Hunting knife 1
Chocolate .... 5 lbs	Pocket knife 1
Cocoa .... 10 lbs	Compass 1
Coffee .... 25 lbs	Awls and tools .... 1 set
Tea .... 10 lbs	Revolver 1
Citric acid .... 1 lb	Rope, ½ or ⅝ inch .... 100 feet
Condensed milk .... 2 doz	Medicine case 1
Soap (laundry) .... 5 lbs	Pitch 1
Soap, toilet (tar) .... 5 cakes	Oakum 1
Matches .... can of 60 pkgs	Fry pan 1
Tobacco, smoking and chewing..	Fish lines and hooks ....
Compressed soups .... 3 doz	Gold scales 1
Compressed soup vegetables.. 10 lbs	Chalk line 1
Bouillon capsules .... 2 doz	Tape line 1
Jamaica ginger (4 oz.) ...... 2 bottles	Money belt 1
Evaporated vinegar .... 1 qt	Cartridge belt 1
Crackers (hard tack) .... 25 lbs	Gold dust bags ....
Stove 1	Snow glasses .... 1 pair
Gold pan 1	Towels 1
Granite buckets, covered 3	Razor 1
Galvanized pails 2	Shaving soap .... 2 cakes

We put up the very best outfits that money can buy.

Everything packed by experienced packers and put up in such a manner that it will reach its destination in perfect order.

COOPER & LEVY

104-106 FIRST AVENUE SOUTH, ONE DOOR SOUTH OF YESLER WAY

ALASKA OUTFITTERS

Form 2134 C.
STEAMBOAT INSPECTION SERVICE.   and Steam

Application for License as Master or Chief Mate of Sail Vessels of Over 700 Gross Tons.

Oct 31st , 1899

To the U. S. Local Inspectors of Steam Vessels,

Port: Seattle Wash.

GENTLEMEN: I, Niels F. D. Jorgensen , hereby respectfully apply for LICENSE as Master and Steam of Sail Vessels of over 700 gross tons.

I am a Naturalized citizen of the United States, over 21 years of age, having been born in the year 1859 at Korsör , in Denmark ; (if foreign born) was naturalized in the U.S.S. Circuit Court at San Francisco in the State of California on the 28 th day of December , 1888, am now a resident of Tacoma , in the State of Washington ; and submit the following statement of my experience and testimonials of character and qualifications:

I have followed the sea for twenty four years of which sixteen years has been in Squarerigged Vessels of which I have been Officer for four Years. I have been Master nearly eight Years, of which six years was in the Schr Glen of San Francisco of which I also was Manager the last two years, fourteen Months in the Schr Dora Bluhm of San Francisco and five Month in Schr F. S. Redfield of San Francisco of which Vessel i am at present Master

And I further say that I have not made application to the Inspector of any other District and been rejected within twelve months of the date of this application.

Sworn to before me this 31 day of Oct 1899

_____ , Inspector.

N F Jorgensen
(City or Town.)

State of _____

WE, THE UNDERSIGNED, DO CERTIFY, from personal knowledge of the above-named Niels F. D. Jorgensen , that he is a person of temperate habits and of good character and recommend him as a suitable person to be entrusted with the duties of the station, as above, for which he makes application.

H C Chesebrough. 48 Market St S.F.
Chas E. Mill Tacoma Wash.
Aug. Fridberg John Annie M. Campbell

NOTICE.—Applicants for license will pay particular attention to the following requirements when filling up this application.
FIRST.—State place and date of application.
SECOND.—State class of license.
THIRD.—In stating experience, give names of vessels, length of time, and in what capacity employed.
FOURTH.—Sign application with full name.
FIFTH.—To be signed only by persons having full personal knowledge of the facts set forth.
Local Inspectors must insist that all the required details in regard to nativity and citizenship are filled out before acting on this application.

2—4033

SHIP'S MASTER LICENSE APPLICATION

When Tacoman Niels Jorgensen filed this application for a license as ship's master, he was required to furnish considerable information to the examining officer about his background and experience. His good character was attested to by three witnesses. We also learn that Jorgensen was forty years of age, was born in Denmark, and had been naturalized as a U.S. citizen in 1888. Jorgensen's application notes that he has "followed the sea for twenty-four years" in square-rigged vessels and in schooners, but his license has penned in the addition "and Steam" to the range of ships in which he applied to be authorized as master. Immigrants like Jorgensen brought vital maritime skills to Puget Sound's waterborne shipping.

GRAND VIEW MENU

This menu from the Grand View Dining Hall in New Whatcom, today's Bellingham, was designed and printed by the Edson and Irish Printing Company. In 1888 John Edson arrived in Bellingham to edit the *Whatcom County Democrat*, and started his own newspaper two years later. Stelle Irish arrived on Bellingham Bay in the statehood year, 1889. Irish and Edson joined forces, and from 1889 through 1906 their firm printed ballots for local elections, calling cards, wedding invitations, theater programs, letterhead stationery, and advertisements of many sorts. The Grand View Dining Hall menu is filled with interesting information about cooking "for ladies and gentlemen" at the close of the nineteenth century, and the fads and fashions of food. The menu's emphasis is on the meal's accompaniments of bread and butter and potatoes, rather than a salad or vegetables. Coffee is the drink of choice, automatically served with every meal. Sardine sandwiches and liver have fallen out of favor with today's diners. A breakfast of "mush and cream" might prepare someone for a morning of heavy labor but seems too rich for our contemporary tastes. "Milk toast" was toasted bread served in warm milk, and became a synonym for someone who was bland and colorless. The prices are startling, but one wonders what was so fancy about the "fancy Porter House steak": the fanciness nearly doubled the price of a garden-variety porterhouse steak. Then as now, oysters, hotcakes, and berries with cream were favorites.

GRAND VIEW DINING HALL

FOR LADIES AND GENTLEMEN

SHORT ORDER BILL OF FARE

Bread and Butter, Potatoes and Coffee served with all Meat and Egg orders

STEAKS AND CHOPS.

Plain Steak	20
Pork Chop	20
Mutton Chop	20
Veal Cutlet	20
" " Breaded	25
Fried Sausage	20
Ham and Eggs	25
Bacon and Eggs	25
Liver and Bacon	20
Liver and Onions	20
Hamburger Steak	20
Corned Beef Hash	20
Sirloin Steak	30
Porter House Steak	40
Fancy Porter House Steak	75

Mushrooms	20
French Peas	20
Spanish Sauce	10
Onions	10

SALADS.

Potato Salad	10
Lobster Salad	20
Shrimp Salad	20

OYSTERS.

Oyster Stew	25
Oyster Fry	35
Pan Roast	35
Oyster Cocktail	10

EGGS.

Fried Eggs	20
Boiled Eggs	20
Poached Eggs on Toast	25
Scrambled Eggs	20
Plain Omelet	20
Ham Omelet	25
Spanish Omelet	25
Oyster Omelet	35

SANDWICHES.

Ham and Egg Sandwich	15
Ham Sandwich	10
Egg Sandwich	10
Sardine Sandwich	15
Roast Beef or Pork Sandwich	10

Hot Cakes with Maple Syrup	10
Buttered Toast	10
Milk Toast	15
Mush and Cream	10
Coffee and Doughnuts	10
Coffee and Cake	15
Bread and Milk	10

All Fruits and Berries in Season.

Bananas and Cream	10
Berries and Cream	10
Sliced Oranges	10

All Vegetables in season served on Ice.

Coffee	5	Tea	5	Milk	5
	Cocoa	10	Chocolate	10	

EDSON & IRISH, PRINTERS, NEW WHATCOM

MARKETING SEATTLE'S TIDELANDS

With the slogan "Business Never Climbs Hills," one of Seattle's preeminent real estate agents set out to celebrate the reclamation of the tideflats. As Seattle's regrading projects moved forward, leveling the city's hills, the "spoils" of the regrade—its rocks, tree stumps, and soil—were used to fill the tideflats so that they were not covered by Elliott Bay at high tide. C. B. Bussell, the author of this 1902 advertising brochure, detailed the explosive growth of warehouses, factories, and docks along this new land, the former tideflats. "Let the thoughtful ones," encouraged Bussell, "be far-sighted enough to avail themselves of the present opportunities while bargains may be had." More important than the brochure's prose, though, is the remarkable image on its cover. Here, a Native couple stares eastward from an island across Elliott Bay at Seattle, a city of smokestacks. Where once there had been a beach, the city's shoreline had become a long boardwalk, punctuated by wharves and docks. The Duwamish people, the people of Chief Seattle, helped build this city but have never been federally recognized. This brochure illustrates their story in the city named for their chief, as much as it does that of the tideflats.

Seattle January 7th 1903.

I Jeremiah Seitzinger of Seattle State of
Washington being of sound mind and
memory do make this my last will and
Testament, Revoking all former wills,
First it is my desire that the persons
and the amounts named herein be paid
First it is my desire that Mrs A C Ryon
of Seattle State of washington be paid
Six Hundred dollars, Second that Mrs
Arthur B Browne be paid Sixty dol-
lars, Third Mr Arthur B Browne
Five Hundred and fifty dollars,
Fourth Annie M Mortimere One dollar
for ungratefulness to her father.
Fifth to Henry C Seitzinger One dollar
for unkindness to his old father, the remain-
-der and residue of whatsoever and wheresoever
it exists, I will and bequeath to my Dauther
Mrs A C Ryan and my Grand daughter Mrs
Arthur B Browne, I also appoint Mrs
A C Ryan and Mrs Arthur B Browne as
my Executors of this will without Bond
they to use the proceeds at their pleasure

Signed & sealed, Jeremiah Seitzinger
in the presence of   X
Geo. Ball
John C Morris

In the Superior Court of the State

FOR THE COUNTY OF KIN

IN PROBATE

IN THE MATTER OF THE ESTATE OF
Jeremiah Seitzinger Deceased.

State of Washington } ss.
County of King

I Mrs Clara Ryan

poses and says: I am the person who he

will and testament of Jeremia

deceased, by the above entitled Court

according to law, the duties of my tru

of Jeremiah

SO HELP ME GOD.

Subscribed and sworn to before me this 18 day of Ju

Herman Shye
Notary Public in and for the State of Washington, residing at Seattle.

No. 4802

IN THE
Superior Court of the State of Washington
FOR THE COUNTY OF KING.

In Probate

In the Matter of the Estate
OF
Jeremiah Seitzinger Deceased

OATH OF EXECUTOR

FILED

Record

JEREMIAH SEITZINGER'S WILL

At the death of Jeremiah Seitzinger, his estate was entered into probate and the executor named in his will, Seitzinger's married daughter Clara Ryan, was sworn to carry out her duties by the clerk of the King County Superior Court. This last will and testament, dated January 7, 1903, revoked all earlier documents and clearly indicated that Seitzinger was "of sound mind and memory." His will is remarkable for its clarity and brevity, and also for its cutting off two children with one dollar each, as punishment of one for "ungratefulness" and of the other for "unkindness to his old father." Seitzinger signed the document with an X, either because he was illiterate or because he was too ill to sign his name.

TRADEMARKS SELL THE SIZZLE

These labels and package designs were trademarked in 1902–03 by innovative entrepreneurs throughout Washington State. As you can see, the sample designs were clipped into files that described the product and its claims, as well as the details of trademark color, size, and so forth. Trademark designs ranged from the eloquent simplicity of McNab's Bed Bug Bane (Spokane) to the elaborate design for Bellingham Bay Brewery, and its three "B's" or bees. Seattle's Reliance brand identified a line of canned foods sold in grocery stores. The perennial preoccupation with health is indicated by the label for curative salts packaged at

Medical Lake, and the "medicinal fluid of vegetable ingredients . . . used as a pain and blood remedy," known as EVO and manufactured in Spokane. The scholar in medieval costume is shown holding a bottle of EVO, the stark black-and-white image trademarked in these documents for use on a label. These trademark files contain dozens of beautiful labels for salmon canned along Washington State's Pacific and Puget Sound coastlines, including Bear Brand fancy hand-packed red sockeye salmon (1902), canned at Henry Newton's cannery in Whatcom County.

SEATTLE TIMES FEATURE

Throughout much of 1905, the *Seattle Sunday Times* ran a series in the rotogravure section entitled "Seattle Women Who Maintain Their Independence." Each week the newspaper celebrated a specific working woman, earning her own way. Five years before Washington State women gained the vote, the newspaper celebrated independent women. Here, Ida Jensen is depicted in a photograph and in a beautifully colored drawing at work making cigars by hand in Michael Wright's cigar factory in Hillman City, in the Rainier Valley. This image was shot directly from the hard copy *Seattle Times*, reminding us that microfilm only captured newspapers in black-and-white. The full-color hard copies have much more to offer, from colorful comic strips to tinted images like this one.

MARGARET RYNO'S DIARY

By their nature, the diaries of ordinary people are filled with pages of, well, *ordinary* events. Throughout Washington, folks kept daily notes about the weather, the work they accomplished, mail they received, and visits from friends and family. Margaret Ryno was a homemaker in Roslyn, whose 1901 diary is clear and legible; the everyday life described in this single page has tremendous charm, marked by her creative spelling of "unveiling," "Alice," and—I think—"verandas." Ryno was a woman of enterprise and energy. Newly arrived in Roslyn from Oklahoma Territory, she mentioned frequent travel—here, to the Teanaway Basin and then to Ellensburg on Sunday for the unveiling of a Woodmen of the World monument. On Monday Ryno papered her dining room, took up the carpet, and did the laundry. Throughout the week, she crafted paper flowers to earn a bit of extra cash. Ryno's son Wallace ("Wallie") worked in the Roslyn coal mines as well as at a variety of odd jobs. On Friday Ryno noted the death of a miner in the Number 2 mine. Less than ten years previously, about fifty miners died at Roslyn in the worst mine disaster in state history, but such death was an everyday matter for Margaret Ryno.

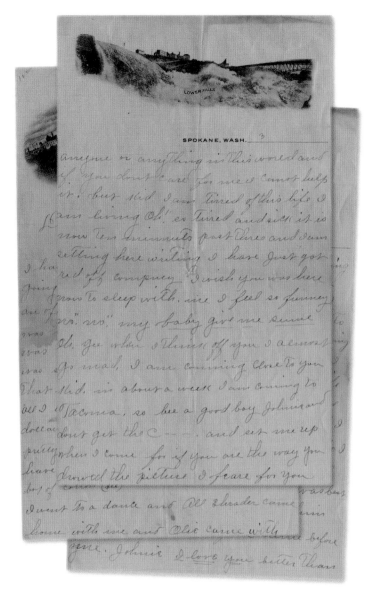

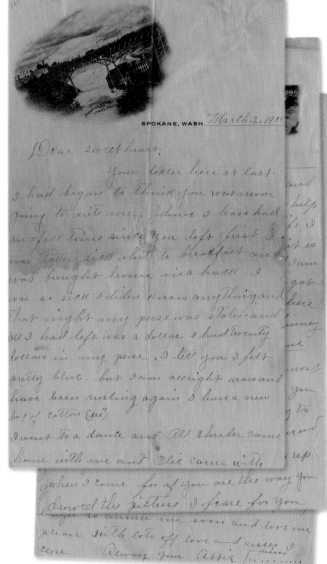

LETTERS
OF A SPOKANE
PROSTITUTE

The Abbie Widner letters comprise a very unusual resource for researching women's history in Washington State. Widner was a prostitute who lived and worked in Spokane's Colonial Hotel in 1905. This remarkable collection consists of three letters from Abbie Widner to her "boy friend," John Weber. Widner was desperately in love with her "Johnie" and eager to be with him, wondering whether she should go "up into the Alaska gold fields" and ply her trade to earn a stake for them both, promising him that "sweetheart, some day we are going to be happy." Her letters expressed her shame and weariness "with this life I am living," and vowed that she wouldn't always be "a sport, so help me God." She once wrote to Weber after "company" had left her, at 3 a.m., tired and sick, drugged with quinine and ergot. Widner's frankness provides us a truly exceptional perspective on vice in Spokane at the beginning of the twentieth century.

AN UNKNOWN COUPLE

Here you see an "Unknown Wedding Couple," from the Albert M. Kendrick Collection. Kendrick was a professional photographer whose life spanned 1896 through 1976, and whose career was based in Ritzville, Adams County, Washington. The Unknown Wedding Couple gaze solemnly into Kendrick's camera, dressed formally for the portrait that marks the beginning of their life together. The wedding and family portraits in this book allow us to study the ways that Washington residents presented themselves to the portrait photographer—how they dressed, how they held themselves, and the importance they attached to the event.

BOOMTOWN TO GHOST TOWN

Today Monte Cristo is a ghost town, at the end of a hike along the old railroad grade. In the mid-1890s Monte Cristo was booming with outside investment, and nearly 2,000 residents hoped to get rich, prospecting in the mountains for gold and silver. The boomtown boasted dozens of hard-rock mining tunnels, a tramway system, an ore concentrator, and the usual gaudy array of saloons. Once the Everett and Monte Cristo Railway opened to carry ore down to the smelter in Everett, the sky seemed to be the limit for the surging boomtown. However, severe flooding along the Stillaguamish River in 1897 badly damaged the railroad, and the ore veins proved to be difficult to work profitably.

When the Klondike Gold Rush began, many raced off to the newest frontier of instant wealth. But the *Everett News* was ever optimistic, so much so that the *Seattle Times* reporter seemed somewhat skeptical of the newspaper's claims of the discovery at Monte Cristo of a "sixteen-inch vein of high-grade tellurides." The 1904 Monte Cristo entry in the *Polk City Directory* is arranged here over the original plat map, filed in 1893. By 1904 the town's population had fallen to a few hundred, but a half-dozen mining companies still employed men as miners and assayers, and the directory hopefully claimed that the surrounding "mountains [are] full of mineral." The mines shut down in 1907.

MARRIAGE RETURN.

[8161]

1. Date of license — Dec. 1st. 1905
2. Full name of groom — Kitaro Arima
3. Age last birthday — 31 yrs.
4. Color (a) — Japanese
5. No. of groom's marriages — First time
6. Residence — Thomas, Wash.
7. Birthplace (b) — Japan
8. Occupation — Farmer
9. Father's name — Heisuke Arima
10. Mother's maiden name — Shiwo
11. Full name of bride — Suyi Arima
    Maiden name if a widow
12. Age last birthday — 18 yrs.
13. Color (a) — Japanese
14. No. of bride's marriages — First time
15. Residence — Japan
16. Birthplace (b) — Japan
17. Occupation — no occupation
18. Father's name — Yasukichi Arima
19. Mother's maiden name — Haya
20. Date of marriage — Dec. 1st. 1905.
21. Place of marriage — S. S. Iyo Maru
22. By whom married, and official station — G. Nakai
    Pastor Buddhist Church, Seattle, Wash.
23. Names of witnesses and their residences:
    No. 1 A. H. Gyffeny, Seattle, Wash.
    No. 2 E. L. Well, Seattle, Wash.

NOTE.—(a) State color distinctly. so race may be known, as White, Black, Mulatto, Indian, Chinese, Mixed White and Indian, etc.
(b) Give state or foreign country, so nationality is plainly shown.

ARIMA MARRIAGE RECORD

This "marriage return" was used to gather personal and statistical data about married couples on their wedding day, including Kitaro and Suyi Arima, on December 1, 1905. Both were born in Japan. The groom was thirty-one years of age and the bride was eighteen—perhaps she was a "picture bride," selected with the help of a matchmaker, photographs, and family connections. The bride and groom were likely to have been relatives since their fathers shared the same surname. The couple was married onboard the *SS Iyo Maru* by the pastor of Seattle's Buddhist Church, and this was probably the ship on which Suyi Arima had traveled across the Pacific Ocean to a wharf in Elliott Bay. The newly married couple then traveled to the groom's farm in Thomas, Washington, south of Kent.

The Okanogan farmer, when he contemplates his season's crop, wears the smile that won't rub off.

IRRIGATING THE OKANOGAN

This political cartoon by Charles Lovejoy appeared in the *Okanogan Record* on August 25, 1905. Lovejoy frequently drew this caricature of a local settler, "the Okanogan farmer," with his characteristic gangly frame, seedy clothing, and crafty, somewhat dissipated expression. Spread behind him was the rich cornucopia of fruit, grain, vegetables, hay, and livestock that would be made possible by the long-anticipated federal irrigation project. Authorized by the Newlands Act, the Reclamation Service—as the U.S. Bureau of Reclamation was then called—began to study irrigation potential in the Okanogan in 1902. The Reclamation Service organized the Okanogan Irrigation District in December 1905 to irrigate nearly 10,000 acres of Okanogan area farmland—the first federal reclamation project in Washington. When Lovejoy drew his cartoon, the project was still under study but was expected to soon be approved; nevertheless, a joined spirit of cynicism and optimism pervades this image.

The Mountaineer

E. L. HAMPTON, Editor.

Application made for entry at the Seattle postoffice as mail matter of the second class.
Subscription price, One Dollar the year. Single numbers Twenty-five Cents.

VOL. 1.　　　　JUNE, 1907.　　　　NO. 2.

RS.

logy and Mineralogy, University of Washington
Dr. J. F. SWEENEY, Member Mazamas
Dr. CORA SMITH EATON, Member Sierra Club
Dr. E. F. STEVENS, Member Mazamas
S, Reference Librarian, Seattle Public Library

DIRECTORS.

HENRY LANDES
W. MONTELIUS PRICE
E. F. STEVENS
J. P. SWEENEY
N YOUNG

TTEES.

Outing.
Mr. Asahel Curtis
Dr. Cora Smith Eaton
Mr. W. M. Price

Publishing.
Mr. E. L. Hampton, Editor
Miss Mary Banks, Associate Editor
Miss Adelaide L. Pollock

THE MOUNTAINEER　　　52

The First Ascent of Mount Shuksan
By ASAHEL CURTIS

MOUNT SHUKSAN, situated in the northern part of Washington, about sixteen miles northeast of Mount Baker, was, so far as we could learn, never climbed until our ascent made in August, 1906.

The mountain is the highest point left of the primary upheaval and is a beautiful mass of igneous rock with cascade glaciers flowing outward on all sides, except the north, from a central snow field. On the northern side of this, and a thousand feet above the snow, rises a great black pinnacle, forming the main summit.

The ascent was attempted first on August 1st by J. A. Lee, Rodney Glisan, E. G. Grinrod, W. M. Price and myself. We followed the ridge that leads to the mountain from the northwest until we were almost directly under the main pinnacle, but were compelled to turn back by an approaching storm, and the lateness of the hour.

Two days later Mr. Price and I attempted the ascent once more, going this time to the south and climbing along the face of the mountain until we came out on top of the main shoulder to the southwest, at an altitude of about 6500 feet, where we spent the night. By means of a rude brush shelter we were able to keep warm although we had no blankets.

On the following morning we continued up the ridge to the snow plateau above the lower pinnacles finding still, to the north, the black mass of the summit pile. The ascent of this rock pile was a rather difficult piece of rock-work that required over two hours.

On the summit we could find no trace of a previous ascent. No rocks had been disturbed, except where the lightning had struck them, and no record had been left. We left a record of the ascent in a glass jar under the cairn that we built, claiming the ascent in honor of the Sierra and Mazama Clubs of which we were members.

The view from the summit should be particularly fine but at this time was hidden by the smoke of forest fires and we could just make out the summit of Mount Baker and a few of the mountains in the range to the north.

51

the main
"Mount S

*Prof
Adv
Comp
Howard,
*Mr. Joh
Com
mers, *M
Dr. Swe
Com
*Mr. Ep
W. H. W
Thos

MT. SHUKSAN.

Copyright 1907 by Romans Photo Co.

ASAHEL CURTIS CLIMBS MOUNT SHUKSAN

In 1906 the Mountaineers was organized to explore and preserve the mountains of Washington State; nearly half the founding members were women. Here we see excerpts from the second issue of the very first volume of *The Mountaineer*, a magazine that is still published today. In June 1907 famed photographer and avid outdoorsman Asahel Curtis reported what he believed to have been the first ascent of Mount Shuksan, just northeast of Mount Baker. Curtis described a rather harrowing ascent of the mountain in August 1906, the previous summer, and lamented that the view from the summit was obscured by the smoke of late summer forest fires. Curtis also described leaving a record of the successful climb in a glass jar, in a cairn of rocks on the summit. His photograph of Mount Shuksan was published in the same issue.

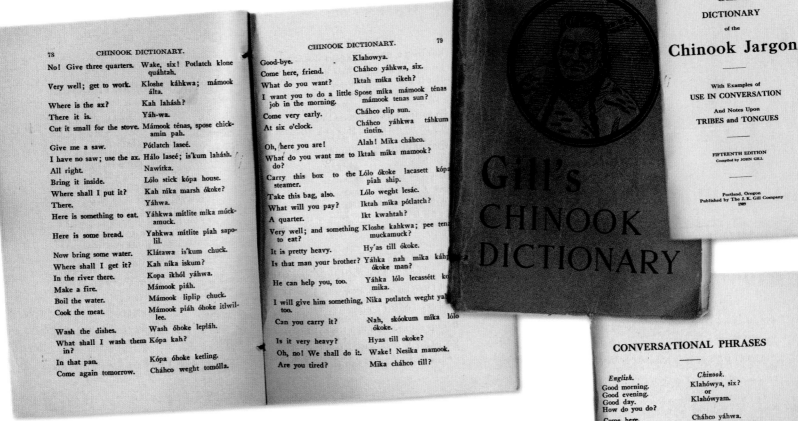

CHINOOK JARGON DICTIONARY

From the moment the archivist at the Cowlitz County Historical Society showed me this copy of the 1909 *Dictionary of the Chinook Jargon*, I knew that the book was extraordinary. Clearly the dictionary had been heavily used. The page edges were stained in the middle where they were thumbed as the owner hunted for words and phrases, either to understand others or to express himself. The dictionary demonstrates that as late as 1909, the Chinook jargon was used to communicate between English speakers and Native people. At some point, the cover became detached from the book and it

was mended at home—reinforced with a heavy fabric impregnated with paste and then rebound with two thick strips of black twine threaded through holes drilled through the book. There was no name written on the blank page at the front, but there was a handwritten list of Chinook words and phrases. This book had been essential to its owner, and as I read, it fell open easily to the excerpted pages, sections that dealt with economic transactions in the mixed society of the early twentieth century, when the owner hired Native people to work for him.

THE MAGAZINE THAT WON EQUAL SUFFRAGE IN WASHINGTON

Votes for Women

VOL. I   SEATTLE, WASHINGTON, DECEMBER 1910   No. 11

UNCLE SAM'S NEWEST GIRL BABY---HE HAS FIVE DAUGHTERS NOW

PROCLAMATION

Whereas, The legislature of the state of Washington, by chapter 18 of the session laws of 1909, submitted to the voters of the state the proposition of amending article 6 of the constitution of said state, the same to be voted upon at the general election to be held on the 8th day of November, 1910; and,

Whereas, It appears from the ballots cast at said election that a majority of the qualified electors voting upon the question of the adoption of said amendment have voted in favor of the same;

Now therefore, I, M. E. Hay, governor of the state of Washington, have proclaimed, and do hereby proclaim, that said amendment has been adopted, and that the same is now a part of the constitution of the state of Washington.

In witness whereof I have hereunto set my hand and caused the seal of state to be hereunto affixed, at Olympia, this 28th day of November, 1910.

WASHINGTON WOMEN VOTE!

On November 8, 1910, the ballot measure to amend the Washington State Constitution to authorize woman suffrage won by a resounding majority of the state's male voters, nearly two to one. The front page of the December 1910 issue of the magazine *Votes for Women* expressed the exultation of victory, celebrating itself as "The Magazine That Won Equal Suffrage in Washington." Five states, all in the West, had by 1910 extended suffrage to women; they are represented in Lulu Shuff's political cartoon as Uncle Sam's five daughters—definitely an odd analysis. An interesting trio of women were depicted visiting Uncle Sam's nursery: first, the flamboyant May Arkwright Hutton, who came from humble beginnings to become a wealthy mine owner and longtime suffragist; second, Mrs. George A. Smith, president of the Alki Point Suffrage Club of Seattle; and third, Katherine MacKay or Mrs. [Clarence] MacKay, a well-known New York suffrage advocate, whose articulate views were often quoted in national magazines. Washington was the first state in the twentieth century to pass women's suffrage, and inspired the national suffrage amendment to the U.S. Constitution, enacted in 1920.

Spokane, Wash., Feb. 10, 1911.

Rev. Anna Shaw,
505 5th Avenue,
New York City.

Dear Miss Shaw:-

Your communication of January 17th I found among an accumulation of mail on my return after a thirty days absence at Olympia, the State Capitol, working in the interest of an eight hour bill for women, which, by the way, will become a law, and some other matters of interest to the women and children in Washington.

With regard to the one cent each from the women of Washington to procure the diamond for the fifth star in the Anthony pin, will say that the sentiment appeals to me but personally I would rather send a check for the entire amount than endeavor to secure it by the one cent process. We of the west seldom waste time over such small amounts besides the newly enfranchised women of the State are busy trying to inform themselves of their duties as newly enfranchised citizens.

If Mrs. Hill takes up the matter I will be glad to personally contribute toward it as she is a woman I have a great deal of respect for both to ability and to honesty of purpose.

Mrs. De Voe and her methods is a stench in the nostrils of every self respected woman in the State. Her star chamber proceedings at Tacoma in organizing the international council of women voters was her latest and I believe greatest farce. The affair has

Miss Shaw -2-

been repudiated by many of the woman's clubs and suffrage organizations, the federation of labor, grange and farmers unions in convention assembled at the State Capitol.

The Seattle women, under the direction of Mrs. Homer Hill, defeated Mayor Gill and his corrupt administration by a majority of 6000 votes. Every newspaper in the State, even those who opposed giving women the ballot conceived that the woman's vote accomplished the result.

On the seventh of March we vote for Commissioners. The morning paper says that more women than men have registered in Spokane for the coming election and they will vote. This noble attitude of the women in accepting the responsibility of the newly acquired duties will do much for suffrage in other States.

I visited at Portland last week. Mr. Charles Piper, editor of the Oregonian (you knew of editor Scott's death) a brother of Senator Geo. Piper who carried our bill through the Washington Senate, told me that if we could get an entirely new element, a new set of Oregon women to take up the cause in that State that the Oregonian would be with them but that the people are tired of the old order of things. He recommended that the subject be dropped for a year or two, in the meantime perfect an organization in which the public would have respect and confidence.

Very respectfully yours for women,

A SUFFRAGIST SPEAKS

On February 10, 1911, May Arkwright Hutton typed this spirited letter to her frequent correspondent, Anna Shaw, in New York. Shaw was the first woman to be ordained as a minister by the Methodist Episcopal Church, and she served as president of the National American Woman Suffrage Association (NAWSA) at the time Hutton wrote this letter. Hutton apologized for her tardy reply, mentioning her own advocacy at Olympia for state legislation to require an eight-hour workday for women, evidence of her lifelong sympathy with and advocacy for working women. Hutton minced no words in her dislike of Emma Smith DeVoe, who had been a professional organizer for NAWSA and also served as president of Washington Equal Suffrage Association. The two women could not have been more different in style: where Hutton was impetuous and ostentatious, even vulgar, DeVoe was polished and ladylike. Both women worked hard toward the same end but in very different ways, and they came into conflict over their 1909 tactics to bring authorizing legislation for the suffrage amendment before the legislature. Hutton also referred with pride to the role that voting women played in the recall of Seattle mayor Hiram Gill, who was considered not only friendly to vice in the city but to be directly profiting from it. She concluded her letter with the good news that Spokane women were taking advantage of their opportunity to vote and shape society, registering to act on "the responsibility of [their] newly acquired duties."

50

DEPARTMENT OF COMMERCE AND LABOR—BUREAU OF THE CENSUS
THIRTEENTH CENSUS OF THE UNITED STATES: 1910—POPULATION

STATE *Washington* • COUNTY *Snohomish* • Township or Other Division of County • NAME OF INCORPORATED PLACE *Everett city* • ENUMERATED BY ME ON THE 15TH DAY OF *April*, 1910. *Joseph Ritton*, ENUMERATOR. SUPERVISOR'S DISTRICT NO. 1 • ENUMERATION DISTRICT NO. 218 • SHEET NO. 12.01 • WARD OF CITY 3

EVERETT, WASH. June 17 190—

Received of EVERETT THEATRE COMPANY

the sum of *One & 00/00* — DOLLARS,

in full payment for services of *Maid* rendered June 17

advertising *Il Trovatore*

Mrs Boyer

Chge

FORUM.

The question box at the Sunday Forum is becoming a most interesting and instructive feature. Last Sunday's questions were answered by Mr. W. C. Peoples in a most thorough manner. Two of the questions, "Is the Negro Benefited by Attending Mixed Schools" and, "Is the Discrimination Against the Negro not Directly Attributable to his Discrimination Against Himself?" brought forth so much discussion that it was decided to continue them for further discussion next Sunday.

Mrs. Boyer, of Everett, will read a paper on the latter question and both will be discussed by the house.

It was also decided to form a bureau of information for our race, so that concerted effort can be made to secure work of all kinds for our people,

Everybody is invited to come out and give an opinion on these two questions.

Mme. Boyer, Everett's leading hair store merchant, spent last Wednesday and Thursday in Tacoma and Seattle. Mme. Boyer, notwithstanding the dull times, reports a very good business outlook. Mr. Boyer is on the road selling goods the most of the time and occasionally she makes short trips out of town and takes a few orders. She is patronized by the leading society ladies of Everett and on the whole has built up a most excellent business.

Mme. Boyer, the well known Afro-American hair dealer of Everett, spent last Thursday in the city. She has a splendid business and is highly pleased with the City of Smokestacks.

Boyden Chester B, mining, h 1621 Rainier av
Boyden Harry, hlpr G N Ry, b 1621 Rainier av
Boyden Joseph, hlpr G N Ry
Boyden Moody, hlpr G N Ry, b 1621 Rainier av
Boye John F, carrier P O, h 3936 Rucker av
Boyer Augustus, foreman pattern shop S I Wrks
BOYER MME LUELLA, Hairdresser and Dermatologist, Hewitt Av, h same, Tels Sunset 1645 Ind 521Y
Boyle David J, mining, h 1831 Colby av
Boyle Dennis P, asst eng E F D, h 2605 Virginia av

OBITUARY

Mrs. Ruth Brent, better known as "Madame Boyer," died last night in Providence hospital following an illness of eleven days. Death came as a result of a complication of disorders.

WHO WAS LUELLA BOYER?

In her day, Luella Boyer was a remarkable woman; today we do not recognize her name and no photograph of her can be found. However, Boyer left a paper trail for the researcher to follow that can bring her back from obscurity. Here you see just a few of the documents that sketch the biography of Madame Luella Boyer, the premier African American businesswoman in Everett at the turn of the twentieth century. The 1910 federal census provides rich documentation for Boyer, then widowed and living with her daughter Esther and a servant. All three were identified as black, and the family was living in a white neighborhood. The 1910 *Everett City Directory* listed Madame Luella Boyer as a "Hairdresser and Dermatologist," with her studio in her home on Hewitt Avenue. A brief article in the August 18, 1905, *Seattle Republican* noted that Boyer was "patronized by the leading society ladies of Everett," and had a "most excellent business." "Mrs. Boyer" signed dozens of receipts for her work as maid at the Everett Theater Company, preparing performers to go on stage. Luella Boyer's active participation in African American social and educational circles was reported in the *Seattle Republican*, the black community's principal newspaper. Her Seattle Sunday Forum presentations are well documented in the *Republican*, and she emerges for us as a thoughtful community organizer. Boyer remarried in 1910, to Bertrand Brent, and her obituary was published on December 17, 1912, in the *Everett Herald*.

Certificate of Marriage No. 16087

CORN/ALFALFA NUPTIALS ANNOUNCED

This Spokane certificate of marriage might easily be passed over as just another public record, one of thousands. However, Certificate No. 16087 acknowledged the solemn nuptials on September 23, 1913, of the groom King Corn and his bride Queen Alfalfa. She was born in Yakima of Asian parents, while he was from Spokane, born of parents from Illinois and Iowa. King Corn was white; his bride, green. His occupation was building up the community, and hers was helping him to do so. This document formalized a stunt to publicize the alternate planting of corn and alfalfa to enrich the soil. At the time Spokane was hosting the Interstate Fair, and enthusiastic proponents of alfalfa had arrived, hoping to introduce Washington State farmers to the alfalfa gospel. September 24, 1913, was declared Alfalfa Day, and Spokane's *Daily Chronicle* reported the evening banquet at which the wedding ceremony took place. G. W. Stocker, one of the certificate's witnesses, stood before the gathering and declared that King Corn had ruined the soil of the Midwest, but "it is said a good woman can reform a bad man and Queen Alfalfa has the virtues and the powers to refertilize and rehabilitate the soil, and to assist King Corn to be more productive."

Greetings from Redmond, Wn.

LAKE SAMMAMISH LUMBER MILL

Labeled "Greetings from Redmond, Wa.," this lovely handmade birthday card was dated May 27, 1911, and its message reads: "Wishing you many happy birthdays. Etta." The card is romantic and impressionistic, its garland of roses embossed and splashed with color; in contrast, the gold trim is uniform—perhaps the uncolored card template was preprinted. The unknown sender, Etta, hand-tinted a photograph of a local lumber mill, perhaps Monohon or Campbell's Mill on Lake Sammamish, placing this industrial site in a rural setting. In the foreground we see floating logs destined for the sawmill; then the smokestacks of the mill, constructed next to a vast barn-like structure and against the rising hillside, covered with timber. By 1911 both Monohon and Campbell's Mill were thriving enterprises.

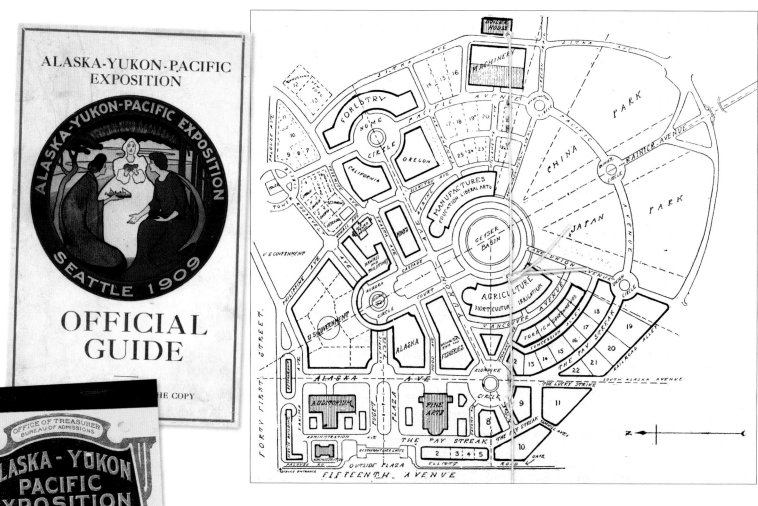

WASHINGTON'S FIRST WORLD'S FAIR

In 1909 Seattle held its first world's fair of the twentieth century—the Alaska-Yukon-Pacific Exposition (AYPE)—to celebrate the explosive growth of the city. The gold rushes to Alaska and to Yukon Territory in Canada, plus trade with China and Japan on the Pacific Rim, had boomed Seattle. The fair was held at the University of Washington, south of the school's handful of buildings, and the elegant Olmsted brothers' design for the fair is evident on the campus to this day. From June 1 through October 16, 1909, more than three million visitors toured the educational exhibits of art and industry, and strolled through the AYPE's acres of gardens. On the Pay Streak, they had their fortune told, took thrilling rides, and paid to see the Incubator Babies and the Igorrote villagers from the Philippines. For more than four months in 1909, the world came to Seattle, and the AYPE marked the city's emergence as the principal city on Puget Sound and as a commanding presence on the Pacific Rim. Visitors wanted to remember the fair and bought souvenirs, photographs, and postcards. Promoters and boosters wanted to remember the fair too, contracting for pamphlets, guidebooks, and a special AYPE newsletter.

X82 Bird's-eye View of the Alaska Yukon Pacific Exposition.

X72 Cascade Court and Arctic Circle from the U. S. Government Bldg.

Official Post Card.

EXPOSITION NUMBER
The Seattle Sunday Times
PART II EIGHT PAGES   Feb. 14th 1909

THE PAY STREAK

Special Music
Offering
Benediction
Report of the committee on Resolutions, which were adopted by the convention.

PREAMBLE

"With deepest gratitude to God for His leadership in the past and with abiding faith for the future, We, the Women's Christian Temperance Union of East Washington in this our 26th annual convention assembled, are sincerely thankful for the growing sentiment which has been crystalized into law in our state; for the favor with which our principles and departmental methods have been received, as shown by our increased membership, and to the splendid state of our finance, and for the progress our cause has made throughout the world. We pledge ourselves to prayerfully labor for the universal adoption of the principles and the prosecution of the methods embodied in the following resolutions:

1st. TOTAL ABSTINENCE—We reaffirm our unfaltering belief in total abstinence from the use of alcoholic liquors, and pledge ourselves anew to the unceasing efforts, that this principle may be firmly established in the habits of life of the people.

2ND. PROHIBITION—With renewed courage and steadfast purpose we again declare our faith in prohibition as the only means of effectually dealing with the traffic in intoxicating liquors and narcotics, and we will not rest until our state has secured a constitutional amendment with adequate law for its enforcement.

3rd. FRANCHISE—Believing in the right of women to express their opinions by the ballot, we will continue to agitate and educate until we secure the enactment of laws that will give suffrage to women on the same terms as men.

4th. PURITY—We will insist upon a single standard of morals for men and women, and will continue to emphasize the existence of nature's inexorable decree that the laws of morality are identical for the two sexes, and this truth must be recognized if the health and vigor of the state is to be maintained. We continue to emphasize the need of wise instruction of children; the enlightenment of men and women as to the results of immorality and the upholding of the highest ideals of purity both within the home and in society.

(B). Deploring the continued existence of the "White Slave Traffic," and the horrible system known as "the segregation and fining of vice," we protest against this infamous business. We will continue to do all in our power to arouse public sentiment until this iniquitous system is abolished. To this end we urge that those who rent property for such vile purposes be ostracised and punished by law, and that officers who will not use their authority for the suppression of vice be retired.

5th. THE FLAG—Inasmuch as the so-called Personal Liberty League stand for the saloon and for the "open Sunday," we protest against the use by that organization of our National flag as its emblem. As patriotic, home-loving women, we believe that the flag, the symbol of freedom, should not be used as the emblem of the lawless enslaving liquor traffic.

6th. BIBLE IN THE PUBLIC SCHOOL—Believing that the Bible contains the principles upon which righteous government is founded, we advocate the reading of the Bible, without comment, in our public schools and other educational institutions.

7th. THANKS—We express our heartfelt thanks to the Woman's Christian Temperance Unions of Spokane for the comfort and enjoyment of the members of this

Where There's Drink There's Danger.   3

Set to music at the request of Miss Frances E. Willard, who wished all young people might commit the words to memory.

ANONYMOUS.   ANNA A. GORDON.
With spirit.

1. Write it on the liq - uor store, Write it on the pris - on door,
2. Write it on the workhouse gate, Write it on the school-boy's slate,
3. Write it on the na - tion's laws, Trampling out the li - cense clause,
4. Write it o - ver ev - 'ry gate, On the church, the halls of state,

Write it on the gin-shop fine, Write, aye write this truth-ful line:
Write it on the cop - y book, Where the young may oft - en look:
Write it on each bal-lot white, So it can be read a - right:
In the heart of ev - 'ry band, On the law of ev - 'ry land;

"Where there's drink there's dan-ger, Where there's drink there's dan - ger."

Senior
Loyal
Temperance
Legion
Song
Book

OF MARCHING SONGS
SERIES No. 4.

BY
ANNA ADAMS GORDON

Secretary of the Loyal Temperance Legion Branch
of the World's Woman's Christian Temperance Union

Price
10
Cents.

MISS RUBY I. GILBERT
Chicago

DEMON RUM

Founded in 1874, the Women's Christian Temperance Union (WCTU) was a national organization by 1909, when Washington women worked toward gaining the vote. Organized to "Agitate—Educate—Legislate," the WCTU advocated total abstinence from alcohol. In 1879 Frances Willard became WCTU's president and poured her intelligence and energy into the reform of American society, attacking a variety of ills with a strategy in which temperance was the integrating tactic. After 1894, under her leadership, the WCTU advocated national woman suffrage, recognizing the power of legislation to enforce social reform. The Eastern Washington WCTU held their annual convention at Spokane's First Baptist Church in 1909, and their preamble and resolutions are excerpted here. Also, from the *Senior Loyal Temperance Legion Song Book*, is one of the WCTU's signature songs, "Where There's Drink, There's Danger"—a beloved old standard by 1909. At Willard's request, her close friend Anna Gordon polished the original anonymous poem and set the words to music. The lyrics clearly express the WCTU's sense that alcohol was at the root of every social problem, destroying families, leading drinkers to prison and the workhouse, and also clearly referring to the political action that would regulate morals and cleanse the nation.

THE APPLE IS THE KING OF FRUIT

YAKIMA ORCHARD SECURITIES CO. NORTH YAKIMA, WASH. U·S·A

1269. Among the Wine Saps, Northern Yakima. Wash.

ₗ Yakima Avenue, one of North Yakima's principal business streets. Substantial structures of brick, modern public utilities, and live, energetic business men are what make North Yakima a progressive city and fully abreast with the times.

YAKIMA—APPLE COUNTRY

This brochure boosted the business prospects and investment opportunities offered by "North Yakima" in 1910. The route of the Northern Pacific Railroad bypassed old Yakima, dealing an apparent death blow to the town's future. But the community rallied and moved more than a hundred buildings north to create a new town on the railroad line, named "North Yakima." The cover of this promotion brochure for North Yakima proclaims that "The Apple is the King of Fruit," and shows the bustling downtown, complete with automobiles and electric streetcar. In 1910 agriculture—and particularly apples—was at the heart of Yakima's prosperity. Beginning in 1906 the Reclamation Service's Yakima Project eventually built six reservoir dams at the headwaters of the Yakima, Tieton, and Naches Rivers, channeling irrigation water to orchards and fields. Over the following century, the lava-rich soil, abundant sunshine, and irrigation turned Yakima-area orchards into large commercial enterprises that ship their fruit by rail to market.

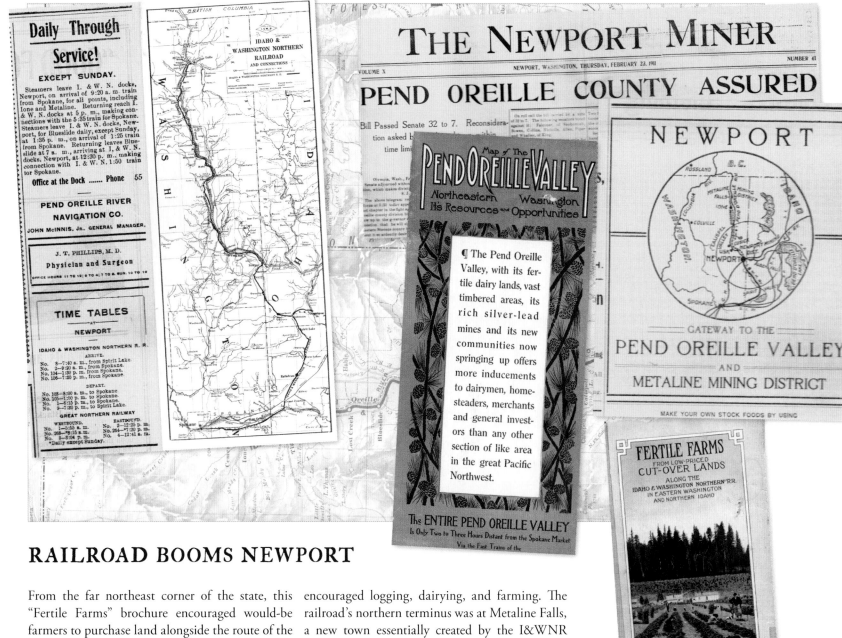

RAILROAD BOOMS NEWPORT

From the far northeast corner of the state, this "Fertile Farms" brochure encouraged would-be farmers to purchase land alongside the route of the brand-new Idaho and Washington Northern Railroad (I&WNR). This land had been clear-cut and was for sale at less than fifty dollars per acre. The completion of the railroad up the valley spurred the split of Pend Oreille County from Stevens County in 1911, the last county to be created in Washington State. The railroad opened up access to the silver-lead mines up the valley, and also encouraged logging, dairying, and farming. The railroad's northern terminus was at Metaline Falls, a new town essentially created by the I&WNR line. These documents celebrate the mining enterprises of the Pend Oreille Valley, as well as the new cement plant to be built at Metaline Falls and the hydroelectric plant then under construction. But it was Newport, the county seat, that became the "Gateway to the Pend Oreille Valley," and the local newspaper—the *Newport Miner*—tracked the town's growth into a little city.

GERTRUD HENRICKSON'S BAPTISMAL CERTIFICATE

This certificate, printed in Swedish, marks the baptism of Gertrud Maria Henrickson, at Coal Creek on March 14, 1919. Born July 2, 1913, she was nearly six years old at her baptism. Late in life, Gertrud Henrickson Glad wrote an autobiography for her family. Her parents had both emigrated from Finland to the Pacific Northwest and wound up in what was then Coal Creek, later called Newcastle. When Glad was a little girl, the Newcastle mines were thriving and hundreds of miners and their families lived nearby. The Seattle and Walla Walla Railroad—recently acquired by the Northern Pacific—provided daily train service to and from Seattle, via Renton. Glad remembered the "new" school, built in 1913, with four classrooms on the main floor and a basement with a home economics kitchen and a manual training shop. In 1921, when she was eight, the Newcastle miners went on strike and her family had to move out of their company house to a temporary camp north of town. They were a union family, and her brother had a paper route, to deliver the Seattle *Union Record*.

ENFORCING MORALITY

In 1914 Washington voters—including women—went to the polls in record numbers, passing an initiative to prohibit "manufacture and sale of intoxicating liquors." The legislation, excerpted below, required that the law be given a "full and fair trial." Temperance advocates hoped to demonstrate that the closure of breweries, taverns, and liquor stores decreased crime, poverty, and domestic violence. Not everyone in Washington was delighted by the experiment: many Washington residents enjoyed picnics at the *biergarten*, a glass of red wine with their pasta, or a few drinks at a party. As Prohibition wore on, statewide efforts to evade it increased, from whiskey stills back in the woods to fast rumrunners on Puget Sound, freighting liquor from Canada to supply illegal speakeasies. Enforcement of temperance proved difficult, as undercover agent H. Lawson's report, below, makes clear. During three days in 1917, he and his partner Lavinsky toured Hoquiam, buying whiskey with ease and jotting surreptitious notes. Lawson kept careful track of his out-of-pocket expenses, in anticipation of reimbursement. One wonders about all those drinks—surely, to remain in character, Lawson and Lavinsky had to manfully down them all. Prohibition in Washington State lasted for more than seventeen years, until federal repeal of the Great Experiment on November 7, 1933.

H. Lawson
AT HOQUIAM   8:30 P. M.

Jan. 16th, 1917

Albert Hotel

Miller,
Jew

3 drinks whiskey, $1.75. Landlady, with big scar
on her right cheek; (2 rounds, 1st paid by Jew,
$.75; second, 4 drinks, paid by me, $1.00. Total
$1.75.)

Jan. 16th, 1917   9:00 P. M.

O'Connor Hotel,

3 rounds whiskey, $3.00
1 bottle whiskey, $2.00
Total, $5.00

Bought of woman proprietress, big Swede, woman
probably of 50 years. Miller and Jew present. I
asked her what her name was, and she said "You
should worry." Old man there called Pete.

816 "J" St.   Jan. 16th, 1917   2:00 P. M.

1 qt. whiskey, $5.00
Paid money to proprietor of boot-black stand at the
bootblack stand. He had another man take us around
to 816 "J" St. This man at 816 "J" St. took us out
to the woodshed and handed us the bottle. Paid
guide $.25, and the man who handed us the bottle
$.25. Total paid, $5.50.

Barber in McKash,   Jan. 18th, 1917   11:30 A. M.
in shop

1 Pt. whiskey, $2.50. Poured it from a quart bottle
into a pint bottle in shop, but made me go out into
the toilet where he delivered same to me. He would
not let both of us go out to toilet when he delivered
bottle and where I paid him the cash.

Present, Lavinsky and Lawson.

Comfort Hotel.   Jan. 17th,   8:20 P. M.

Mr. Lavinsky and myself went to Comfort Hotel, purchased 2 rounds of drinks, paying him $.50 a round.
Total, $1.00.

I certify that the foregoing statement is of intoxicating
liquor purchased by me at the several dates mentioned and from the
several persons and in the amounts, and that I paid the several amounts
set down for the same.

Jan. 20th, 1917.

H. LAWSON.

In the House   By R. Reeves

HOUSE JOINT RESOLUTION NO. 2

STATE OF WASHINGTON, FOURTEENTH REGULAR SESSION.

January 14, 1915; read first and second time, ordered printed,
and referred to Committee on Public Morals.

Providing that this legislature declare its determination not to
consider or enact any bill or measure whatsoever dealing with
or relating to the liquor traffic, or submitting or resubmitting in any form anything purporting to amend, modify or
supersede the existing enactment of the people by Initiative
Measure No. 3.

WHEREAS, The people of Washington, by decisive vote on
November 3rd, 1914, have regularly enacted Initiative Measure No.
3, providing for statewide prohibition of the manufacture and
sale of intoxicating liquors for beverage purposes, which said
measure becomes fully effective on January 1, 1916; and

WHEREAS, The will of the people upon this question was
expressed after a long and thorough campaign which aroused public
interest to the extent of bringing out a total vote one-sixth
larger than the previous high record vote at the last presidential
and state election, and was further emphasized by the fact that
the total vote upon this question exceeded by more than 25,000
votes the total cast on the same day for all the candidates for
United States senator, and by more than 50,000 votes the total cast
for members of this legislature in all the combined districts of
the state; now, therefore,

BY IT RESOLVED, BY THE LEGISLATURE OF THE STATE OF WASHINGTON:

That in obedience to the will of the people, expressed by
decisive majority of an unprecedented total of the state electorate,
in the enactment by direct vote of a law thoroughly and completely
dealing with the traffic in intoxicating liquors, this legislature
does hereby declare its determination not to consider or enact
any bill or measure whatsoever dealing with or relating to the
said liquor traffic; or submitting or resubmitting in any form
anything purporting to amend, modify or supercede the existing
enactment of the people, thereby permitting the new law, enacted
by the direct vote of the people to have a full and fair trial,
according to the true spirit of American institutions and praticu-
larly applying in letter and in spirit the provisions of our state
constitution providing for the initiative and referendum.

Department of the Interior,
Mt. Rainier National Park,
Carbon River Ranger Station,
Fairfax, Wash., July 29, 1915.

Mr. D. L. Reaburn,
Supervisor, Mt. Rainier National Park,
Ashford, Wash.

Dear Sir:

On my trip to Glacier Basin and the eastern boundary of the park on the 26th, while passing through Yakima Park I found the remains of an Indian camp where the bands of natives are accustomed to annually make visits for the purpose of hunting deer. They have constructed two corrals for their horses by cutting down timber and also a wigwam of poles. There are great quantities of bones and other evidences of recent game destruction. I wish to be advised as to whether or not the Indians under their treaty with the federal Government have the right to hunt and take game in National Parks and if not what steps are to be taken to cause a discontinuance of this practice.

Yours very respectfully,

Thomas O'Farrell
Park Ranger.

DLR
Enumclaw
Aug 29-15

Mr Reaburn
Ashford
Was

Dear Sir
I am writing you in regards to the Indians hunting in the Park. I meet a few last wensday 25th & tried to explain to them the rules of said Park but they wouldn't listen to me & they also had card & letter dated from 1878 to this present date & the old chief Sluskin the Chief of the Yakimas

said he intended to hunt & kill when & where he wanted to but would not slaughter any more than they needed I would like to be informed about this matter as soon as possible for they are still in the park.

Yours truly
Park Ranger Arthur White
Enumclaw
Wash

DEPARTMENT OF THE INTERIOR
WASHINGTON

ADDRESS ONLY
THE SECRETARY OF THE INTERIOR

AUG -9 1915

Dear Mr. Reaburn:

Your letter of August 2, enclosing one addressed to you by Park Ranger O'Farrell, relative to hunting depredations by Indians within the park has been received.

In reply you are advised that the act of Congress establishing Mount Rainier National Park makes no provision for hunting therein by Indians. In order to determine whether or not any rights under treaty are involved in the hunting by particular Indians, it would be necessary that we know to what tribe the Indians belong. If this information can be procured and forwarded, an effort will be made to answer your question more definitely.

Cordially yours,

Ayers
Acting Assistant Secretary.

Mr. D. L. Reaburn,
Supervisor, Mount Rainier National Park,
Ashford, Washington.

TREATY RIGHTS, 1915

These three pieces of correspondence document encounters in 1915 between Mount Rainier National Park rangers and a band of Yakama hunters, led by Chief Sluiskin. During a wide-ranging trip along the park's eastern boundary, Ranger Thomas O'Farrell found the remains of an Indian hunting camp and wrote to ask his supervisor, DeWitt L. Reaburn, for guidance. Did these Indians, their tribe unspecified by O'Farrell, "under their treaty with the federal government, have the right to hunt and take game in National Parks?" And, if they didn't, what steps should O'Farrell take? Reaburn wrote to his own boss at the Department of the Interior, in Washington, DC. The bureaucratic machine ground along slowly and uncertainly. Park Ranger Arthur White also encountered the band of Yakama hunters, and informed them of "the rules of said Park, but they wouldn't listen to me." Instead, Sluiskin showed White paperwork dating from 1878 authorizing the hunt, which, of course, was guaranteed by the original treaty. These three documents leave the matter inconclusive, but six Yakama hunters were arrested two seasons later in the park for hunting deer.

SOCIALISM IN COWLITZ COUNTY

In 1901 the Socialist Party of Washington was formed, joining threads that led forward from a number of independent labor, populist, and socialist initiatives, as well as from experiments in utopian communal life. Plagued by bitter factionalism, Washington's Socialists nevertheless mustered nearly eight percent of the votes cast in the state for the 1908 presidential bid of Eugene Debs. Below, Kelso's *Socialist News* published a front-page op-ed piece in 1917, railing against card-carrying Socialists who had voted for Democrat Woodrow Wilson for president, betraying their own class interests. "No one," wrote the editor, "expected to elect [Allan L.] Benson president at this election," but it was vital that Socialists stick together and show their strength. Later in the spring, the Socialist Party in Kelso held a dance at McDonough Hall and published this poster to invite the crowd. In the logging camps and milltowns of Western Washington, the Socialist Party remained powerful among laboring men and their families.

A DOUGHBOY WRITES HOME

Shown here is one of the letters between Jake Schomber and Minnie Wilson—the first that he wrote to her while stationed in France. They had grown up together in Issaquah and planned to marry. Schomber was a "Doughboy," drafted as a member of the American Expeditionary Forces, and his letter was stamped "On active service with the U.S. Naval forces operating in European waters." Schomber initially mustered in at Camp Lewis—today's Fort Lewis—and he also referred in his letter to Camp Fremont, in California, where his unit was trained in boot camp. By May 1918 nearly one million American soldiers were on duty in Europe, and of that number about 50,000 died of battle injuries. An additional 25,000 soldiers died in the influenza pandemic. Here, Schomber wrote to Minnie from Brest, France, nearly a month after the armistice was signed, describing his trip across France in a troop train and his stay at the very camp where "Napolion" trained his own infantry. Schomber was lucky and returned to Issaquah to marry his Minnie and enjoy a long life with her. The letter clearly shows Jake Schomber's optimistic personality, gritty common sense, and ad hoc spelling.

WISH YOU WERE HERE...

Tacoma Public Library's online collection of postcards offers a delightful experience to the browsing researcher. A handful of examples are spread on these two pages. Drawn from throughout the state, these postcards express the earnest boosterism and folksy humor of the early twentieth century. Although a few were mailed from tourists on their travels, many more were sent by friends and family to the folks back home.

ORDINANCE
No. 38971

AN ORDINANCE relating to the public health, declaring Influenza to be a quarantinable disease, providing for the quarantine thereof and the promulgation of quarantine regulations, and providing penalties for the violation thereof, and declaring an emergency.

SEATTLE, WASHINGTON

1918

ORDINANCE No. 38971

AN ORDINANCE relating to the public health, declaring Influenza to be a quarantinable disease, providing for the quarantine thereof and the promulgation of quarantine regulations, and providing penalties for the violation thereof, and declaring an emergency.

Be it ordained by the City of Seattle as follows:

Section 1. It shall be unlawful for any physician, nurse, practitioner or healer, or any other person pretending to act as such, attending, treating or prescribing any treatment, medical or otherwise, for any other person sick with the disease commonly known as influenza, or showing symptoms thereof; or, in case there be no such person attending, treating or prescribing, for the head of any household or proprietor of any hotel or lodging house, hospital, or sanitarium, having reason to believe that an inmate of his establishment is afflicted with said influenza, to fail, neglect or refuse to immediately report in writing to the Commissioner of Health of the City of Seattle the existence of such influenza, and the name and location of the person afflicted or showing symptoms of being afflicted therewith; provided, that it shall be a sufficient defense in any prosecution under the provisions of this section that such report was timely made by any other person.

Section 2. It shall be unlawful for any person, knowing or having cause to believe himself to be sick with influenza, to appear upon any of the streets, alleys or other public places of the City of Seattle, or move about or approach or mix with other persons, or to move to or visit another habitation or building, or to remove from any house or place to any other house or place, or leave any such house or place for any purpose, or for any person to remove any such sick person from any such house or place to any other house or place, or for any person living in the house with any such sick person to leave such house, without permission from the Commissioner of Health so to do.

Section 3. That the disease commonly known as influenza be and hereby is declared to be a dangerous, contagious and infectious disease and subject to quarantine as such, and the Commissioner of Health of the City of Seattle is hereby empowered and authorized, whenever he shall deem it necessary for the protection of the public health, to promulgate and enforce all necessary quarantine rules and regulations in relation thereto.

Section 4. Nothing herein shall be deemed to repeal, change, alter, or affect any of the terms or conditions of any of the existing ordinances of the City of Seattle in relation to public health, and the terms and conditions of this ordinance shall be deemed to be cumulative to and of existing ordinances.

Section 5. Any person violating or failing to comply with any of the provisions of this ordinance, or of any of the provisions of the rules or regulations of the Commissioner of Health of the City of Seattle made pursuant thereto, shall be deemed guilty of a misdemeanor, and upon conviction thereof shall be punished by a fine in any sum not exceeding one hundred dollars ($100.00), or by imprisonment in the city jail not exceeding thirty (30) days, or by both such fine and imprisonment.

Section 6. By reason of the existence of an epidemic of influenza within the City of Seattle, immediate action is necessary for the preservation of the public health, Now, therefore,

Section 7. By reason of the facts set forth in this ordinance an emergency is declared to exist; therefore this ordinance shall take effect and be in force from and after its passage and approval by the Mayor.

Passed the City Council the 5th day of December, 1918, and signed by me in open session in authentication of its passage this 5th day of December, 1918.

T. H. BOLTON,
President of the City Council.

Approved by me this 5th day of December, 1918.

OLE HANSON
Mayor.

Filed by me this 5th day of December, 1918.

Attest:　　　　　　H. W. CARROLL,
City Comptroller and ex-officio City Clerk.

(Seal)　　　　　　By E. M. STREET,
Deputy Clerk.

INFLUENZA EPIDEMIC

On December 5, 1918, the Seattle City Council passed ordinance No. 38971 in response to the influenza epidemic then raging in the city. The ordinance required that all cases be immediately reported to the commissioner of health, and stipulated that anyone with the symptoms of influenza be quarantined and not "move about or approach or mix with other people . . . or leave [his/her] house or place for any purpose." The city was in crisis. The city council declared that influenza was a "dangerous, contagious and infectious" disease and extended extraordinary powers of enforcement, including jail time and heavy fines. For five weeks Seattle schools and theaters were closed, and many citizens wore paper or fabric masks to protect against contagion. Nearly every day, influenza deaths were reported in Seattle's newspapers, and—worldwide—the death toll of the pandemic rose to nearly forty million.

THE CHATTERS
FAMILY

In about 1925 John and Gertrude Chatters, along with their children Iva and Owen, posed for a studio photographer in Seattle. Dressed in their best, they gaze at us across the years with a quiet calm.

Thos. H. Tracy   Age 36   No.4866
Alias Geo. Martin

SOLIDARITY FOREVER!
By Ralph H. Chaplin
(Tune: "John Brown's Body")

When the Union's inspiration through the worker's blood
    shall run,
There can be no power greater anywhere beneath the sun.
Yet what force on earth is weaker than the feeble
    strength of one?
        But the Union makes us strong.

CHORUS:
Solidarity forever!
Solidarity forever!
Solidarity forever!
But the Union makes us strong.

Is there aught we hold in common with the greedy para-
    site
Who would lash us into serfdom and would crush us with
    his might
Is there anything left for us but to organize and fight?
        For the Union makes us strong.

It is we who plowed the prairies; built the cities where
    they trade.
Dug the mines and built the workshops; endless miles of
    railroad laid.

Now we stand, outcast and starving, 'mid the wonders we
    have made;
        For the Union makes us strong.

All the world that's owned by idle drones, is ours and ours
    alone.
We have laid the wide foundations; built it skywards,
    stone by stone.
It is ours, and not slave in, but to master and to own,
        While the Union makes us strong.

They have taken untold millions that they never toiled to

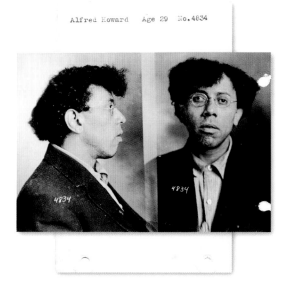

Alfred Howard Age 29 No.4834

Adolph Erson Age 26 No. 4832

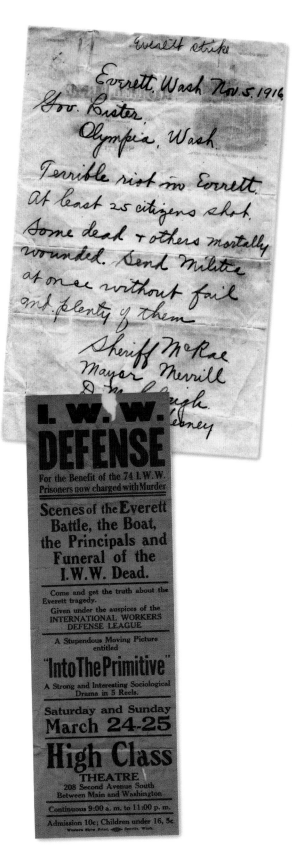

SOLIDARITY FOREVER

The Industrial Workers of the World—the Wobblies—were established in Chicago in 1905, but quickly spread to the mines, sawmills, and logging camps of the Pacific Northwest. In Washington, the Wobblies were most successful among footloose men working in harsh conditions, and their message was powerful: labor and management have nothing in common—the laboring class is the productive class; one big union and one big strike are needed to break the capitalist system. The Wobblies argued against service in World War I, interpreting it as a "rich man's war for poor men to fight," a conflict in which laboring men had no stake. This revolutionary message is graphically represented by the poster entitled "The Pyramid of the Capitalist System," which shows the men and women whose labor supports the layers of society. Unlike the American Federation of Labor, the "one big union" did not discriminate against unskilled, nonwhite, or female workers: anyone could join, gain a membership card, and sing "Solidarity Forever." Three years before the 1919 Armistice Day parade in Centralia and Seattle's General Strike, the Everett Massacre took place. On November 5, 1916, 250 Wobblies steamed to Everett from Seattle on the *Calista* and *Verona*, to protest the beating of Wobblies by Everett vigilantes. When the *Verona* docked, the Wobblies were met by nearly two hundred armed deputies. The ensuing gun battle on Bloody Sunday left two deputies and at least five Wobblies dead. Everett's mayor, [Dennis] Merrill, and sheriff, [Donald] McRae, and industrialists [David] Clough and [John] McChesney signed the letter to Governor Ernest Lister, requesting militia protection. On their return to Seattle, seventy-four Wobblies were arrested for murder; you see three of them in these photos: Thomas H. Tracy, Alfred Howard, and Adolph Erson. All were eventually released except Tracy, who was charged with the murders of deputies Jefferson Beard and Charles Curtis. Following a dramatic and much-publicized trial, Tracy was acquitted.

YAMADA WEDDING COUPLE

In 1922 Masato and Suzue Yamada posed for a formal wedding portrait. Their wedding ceremony was held at the White River Buddhist Temple in Auburn, Washington. The Yamadas later owned a grocery store in Kent.

Seattle Times Nov. 14, 1924

MOUNT RAINIER? OR NOT?

These three clippings concern the 1924 controversy over the naming of Mount Rainier—a longstanding dispute kept at a fever pitch by Tacomans. U.S. senator Clarence Dill and U.S representative Albert Johnson, both from Washington State, had introduced bills in their respective houses to change the mountain's name "back to the original Indian appellation," Tacoma. "Rainier," they claimed, commemorated a British naval officer, a "second-rate enemy admiral." The Sam Armstrong cartoon—undated and unsourced—clearly espoused the Tacoma point of view, as did the editorial "The Mountain's Name." Both the editorial and cartoon were certainly published in a Tacoma newspaper, likely the *Tacoma News Tribune*, in late 1923 or 1924. The tart remarks of the U.S. Geographic Board in rejecting unanimously for the fourth time this change of Mount Rainier to Mount Tacoma were dotted with exclamation marks, and condemn the "propaganda from Tacoma . . . carried on over a series of years."

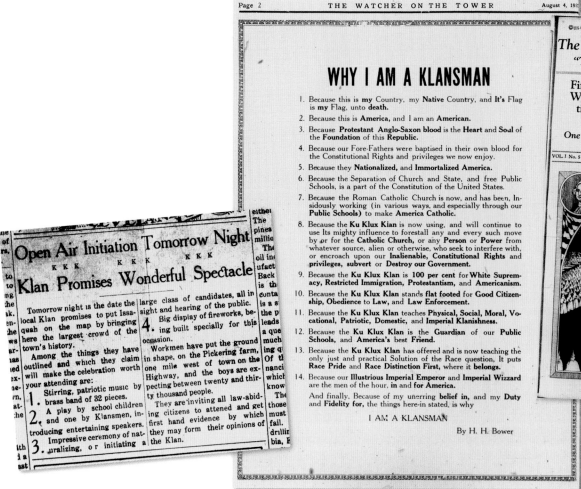

WASHINGTON'S KU KLUX KLAN

The revival of the Ku Klux Klan in the 1920s—the Second Klan, as it is often called—is a major story in Washington State. The *Watcher on the Tower*, published in Seattle, was a slickly produced and carefully edited magazine, and the article "Why I Am a Klansman" leaves no doubt that this organization was not merely a social club but a white supremacist, anti-Catholic organization of domestic terrorism. The July 21, 1923, *Watcher* cover described a "vast ceremony" at Wilson's Station, south of Seattle, where fifty thousand Klansmen and friends witnessed the initiation of nearly two thousand new members. The following summer, a reporter for the *Issaquah Press* estimated that fifty-five thousand had assembled for a Klan event on the Pickering Farm a mile west of town. Throughout the evening, an electrical forty-foot-tall "fiery cross" was illuminated on the grounds, and the program included music by a brass band, plays, and tableaux, plus a grand finale of fireworks. The highlight of the evening was the initiation of 250 new Issaquah Klansmen, under the guidance of Exalted Cyclops T. N. T. Evans.

HITT FIREWORKS

The Hitt Fireworks Company was founded in 1905 and became a longstanding business in Seattle's Rainier Valley, up on Hitt's Hill. Hitt did not just produce individual fireworks like the "Flashcracka," but also orchestrated fireworks tableaux and displays for major clients. Before and after the Hitt Company's short-lived merger with the Victory Fireworks Company, the firm designed dramatic firework displays for the 1909 Alaska-Yukon-Pacific Exposition in Seattle, the San Francisco Panama-Pacific International Exposition in 1915, and the Philadelphia Sesquicentennial International Exposition in 1926. Their last major show was the 1974 Seattle Fourth of July fireworks, sponsored by Ivar's. Hitt's beautiful and dramatic promotional materials truly convey the joy of fireworks exploding against the dark night sky.

RIEL WEDDING COUPLE

On April 10, 1929, Leonide Riel and Florine Patnode were married in Moxee, Washington. Moxee had attracted generations of French and French-Canadian farmers, and the Riels were likely married by a French-speaking priest at Holy Rosary Parish.

FOREST PRODUCTS BRAND

Know all Men by These Presents: That *Oxenford Bros.*

_____, of the city of *Port Angeles*

County of *Clallam*, State of *Washington*, has heretofore adopted and does hereby adopt the following mark or brand, and does hereby make application for the registration of said mark or brand in the office of the Secretary of State of the State of Washington, said mark or brand being described as follows, to-wit:

The letter B in a circle.
The B is connected to the Circle at the top and Bottom. The circle is 2½ inches outside Diameter
B in Center is 1½ inches long
Width of line on circle is about 3/16. On B about ⅛ inch

Make drawing of mark or brand here:

as shown by the accompanying facsimiles or counterparts thereof, filed herewith, which are true and correct copies of said mark or brand. The article on which this mark or brand is to be used is *Logs, Poles, Piling, Bolts, Ties and Forest Products of every description*

Such mark or brand at the time of adoption was not in use by any other person, firm or association, I verily believe and this mark or brand is selected in good faith for marking or branding forest products, and no other person, firm, association, union or corporation has the right to such use, either in the identical form or in any such near resemblance thereto as may be calculated to deceive.

Oxenford Bros
per M Schmitt

Subscribed and sworn to before me this *17* day of *June*, A. D. 192*6*

Notary Public in and for the State

of *Washington*

residing at *Olympia*

[Impress Seal here]

LUMBER BRAND

Throughout Washington, registries of stock brands form part of the collection at the branches of the Washington State Archives (WSA). Some of the very oldest are held at the WSA-Eastern Region, Cheney and at the WSA-Central Region, Ellensburg. However, this brand, registered in Clallam County in 1926, was not a brand for hogs, steers, or sheep—rather, it was a brand for lumber of every sort produced by the Oxenford Brothers Company, based in Port Angeles.

CASCADE CURTAIN

Throughout Washington history, first the Columbia River and then the Cascade Mountains have suggested a barrier and a boundary. The Cascade Tunnel Association published this leaflet in 1930, arguing for an automobile tunnel to be bored through the North Cascades along Route 2, from Leavenworth to Skykomish. At that time, snow and the threat of avalanches closed Route 2 for five months each year, and proponents believed that this tunnel—nearly thirty miles in length—would advance Washington State commerce by connecting the Eastern Washington "loop highway" to Western Washington. Austin E. Griffiths, president of the Cascade Tunnel Association, had a longstanding interest in opening Washington State to year-round tourism and commerce. Never built, the Cascade Tunnel is one of a number of interesting unbuilt projects: filling in Seattle's Lake Union; constructing bridges among the San Juan Islands; and boring a tunnel through Beacon Hill in Seattle, to connect Lake Washington and Elliott Bay.

THE ENG FAMILY

In 1927 Mr. and Mrs. Sam Choi Eng and their children posed for the photographer. Mr. Eng and the children are dressed in Western clothes, but Mrs. Eng wears a more traditional Chinese costume.

TRADEMARKS SELL MORE SIZZLE

Here are a handful of the trademarks registered by Washington entrepreneurs between 1925 and 1929, from registrants throughout the state. Many Seattle folks remember Frye's Packing Plant and the great fire of February 18, 1943, when the super-secret B-29 Superfortress crashed into the plant on a test run. Here is a label from Frye's sausage and a label for Frye's packaged mincemeat. Yakima potatoes were sold with the Washington brand on their burlap bags. In Spokane, Cambern's Dutch Shops offered a variety of grocery items, all identified by the little Dutch maid. Similarly, in Centralia, Colson's marketed a number of grocery items under this label—here we see the Honey Nut Spread—and Tacoma's Federal Bakery registered the Marvel brand for its baked goods.

THE HUNGRY
THIRTIES

In the flyer to the left, the Spokane County Unemployed League announced a march through the city to demand support for the unemployed from the county commissioners. "It ought not," the flyer maintained, "take a bloody revolution" to get food for the unemployed. The Great Depression hit the mines, woods, mills, orchards, and fields of Washington very hard, and unemployment averaged close to 30 percent throughout the state. One of the "bankers and unprincipled usurers" referred to in the flyer might have written the 1932 poem mailed to the Washington Emergency Relief Administration, excerpted below, protesting any relief for the jobless. In the poet's view, "the bunch of hobos" had been reckless and irresponsible during the good times, then demanded "tobacco and food, gasoline and shelter" when times were tough, while despising the hardworking "saps" who support them.

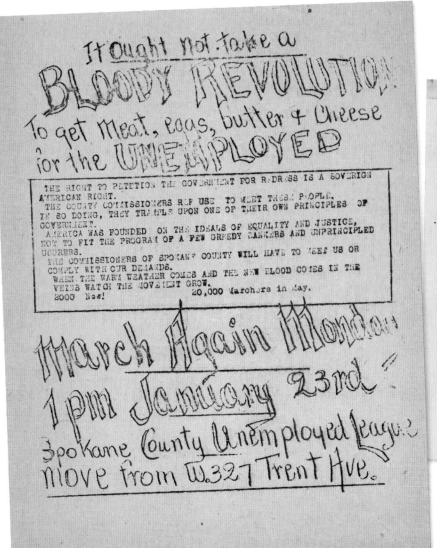

Hark! Hark! The autos bark,
The beggars are coming to town,
Some with a smile, our cash to beguile
And some with an ugly frown.

They blew all they made when times were fair,
And now they demand everything free as air,
Free tobacco and food, gasoline and shelter,
Or they say they'll knock things helter skelter.

They live on you and they live on me
As they stuff and guzzle our grub so free.
For our forced contribution, do they give us thanks?
No - they grab all they can and call us cranks.

So stuffing, and puffing a free cigar,
They roll along with free gas in their car.
Free gas in their car and free grub in their belly,
And they wish you and I were smashed to a jelly.

And aren't we the saps to come through so easy
To a bunch of hobos, lazy and greasy?

MULLIGAN STEW

Ronald D. Ginther's ink-and-watercolor drawings offer an unflinching study of the homeless, jobless poor of the Great Depression. Ginther depicted Salvation Army revival meetings, soup kitchens, police brutality, revolutionary street-corner gatherings, jail scenes, Hooverville, and the miseries and indignities of everyday life among the destitute. Here we see a group of hobos in a clearing near Seattle cooking up a mulligan stew of food they've foraged and stolen from nearby farms. Behind them passes a freight train, with more men riding the boxcars to or from Seattle, or perhaps preparing to jump off and join this homeless camp. Ronald Debs Ginther was born in 1904, and was given his middle name to honor Socialist Eugene V. Debs. As a young man, Ginther joined the Industrial Workers of the World (the Wobblies). During the Great Depression, he "worked when he could and bummed around when he couldn't," his son reminisced. A self-taught artist, Ginther spent time in the places and with the people that became the subject of so many of his paintings.

WPA PROPERTY RECORD CARD

The remarkable collection of Real Property Record Cards, originally created by the King County Assessor's Office, is distinguished by the photos taken by the federal Works Progress Administration (WPA), a New Deal program, between 1937 and 1940. The cards contain information on individual parcels of property, including legal descriptions, some building history, building types and uses, number of rooms, construction details, and at least one photograph of the major structure on the parcel. The cards also contain the assessed valuation for each parcel of property for the period from about 1937 until 1972, when the cards were replaced by an automated database. This collection is an excellent example of the changing uses of records: contemporary researchers use the cards to find historic photos of their homes or businesses, if they were built during or prior to the WPA project, but the records were originally created to properly assess King County property taxes. Here we see the Real Property Record Card and photographs for Seattle's Twin Teepees, near Green Lake on Aurora Avenue North, a roadside attraction that was brand-new in 1937.

JOINING THE CCC

Of all the New Deal programs initiated by President Franklin Delano Roosevelt, the Civilian Conservation Corps (CCC) gained the widest popular support. The CCC put young men, aged eighteen to twenty-five, to work on conservation projects throughout the United States. In Washington State they fought fires; cleared trails; controlled erosion; and built irrigation dams and ditches, campgrounds, and fire towers. The CCC was a quasi-military organization, registering young men in companies and housing them in disciplined camps in remote areas. Each worker received thirty dollars per month, of which twenty-five was sent home to his family. Here you see excerpts from

Thomas D. Noonan's personal copy of the *Hysterical History*, a CCC yearbook for his unit, which was assigned to the Tahoma Creek camp near Narada Falls. The book included autographs from Noonan's friends and his own memories of his unit and their hard work on Mount Rainier. Noonan joked that his work consisted mostly of K.P. (Kitchen Privileges) and building trails, and that his fun was dancing, necking, and drinking. The cartoons on the cover and inside show the very simple CCC uniform, and the slightly risqué humor of the CCC "boys," away from mom and dad for the first time and meeting young women at local dances.

NEW DEAL ART

In 1934 Ernest Ralph Norling drew this pencil sketch of a group of CCC men hard at work on Orcas Island, building a hiking trail through the woods. Norling was assigned to document the CCC in an early New Deal program to employ American artists, the Public Works of Art Project, which ended in June 1934 and was succeeded by the better-known Federal Art Project. Norling was active into the early 1960s, illustrating a series of books with his wife, Jo Norling, and others, and writing how-to books for amateur artists, many of which are still in print.

NORTHWEST'S COLUMBIA BASIN PROJECT

The Columbia Basin Project was a mammoth program of land reclamation, irrigation, and production of hydroelectricity—a New Deal project designed to reinvent Washington State. The construction of Grand Coulee Dam, key to the Columbia Basin Project, began in 1933 and was not completed until 1942. The Bonneville Power Administration was organized to manage the hydroelectricity generated by the dams on the Columbia River. This cheap electricity powered the World War II home front production of aluminum, bombers, and pluto-

nium. The Project is the largest federally run irrigation project in the United States, bringing water to nearly 700,000 acres. Additionally, Grand Coulee dam generates an average annual net of about 21.2 billion kilowatt-hours of electricity. This terrific 1934 map clearly shows the regional integration of the Project, as its impacts spread throughout the Pacific Northwest. This map is also interesting for what *didn't* exist in 1934: there is no North Cascades Highway, no Hanford Nuclear Reservation, and Mount St. Helens is still whole.

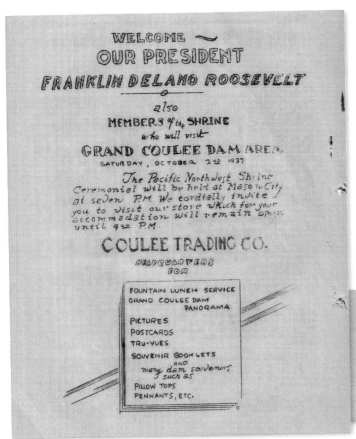

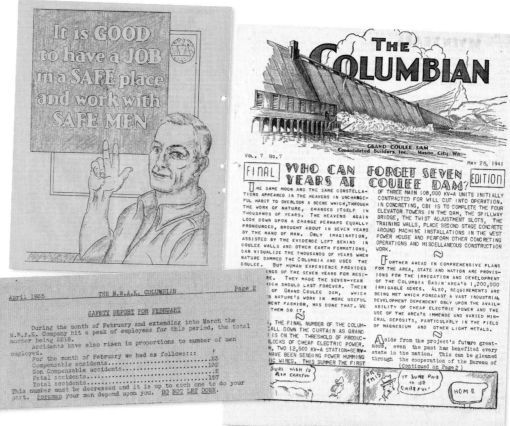

BUILDING GRAND COULEE DAM

Construction of Grand Coulee Dam was a spectacular civil engineering achievement that transformed Washington State; it also dislocated Native people, dramatically altered the environment, and destroyed upriver salmon-spawning grounds. In 1934, at the project's beginning, the successful construction bid was submitted by a consortium of companies: Silas Mason, Walsh Construction, and Atkinson-Kier, popularly known as M.W.A.K. The *M.W.A.K. Columbian* was the newspaper produced for the workers, and the publication emphasized safety on this extremely dangerous and complex job. Over the years, as the workforce climbed past seven thousand, cartoons and slogans discouraged haste, carelessness, and horseplay. All told, seventy-seven men died building Grand Coulee Dam. The New Deal Public Works Administration managed the project, and the dam's payroll became the largest in the nation. In the depths of the Great Depression, housing was built at Engineers Town on the west side of the river, and on the east side Mason City housed a population of three thousand workers and their families. The town of Grand Coulee incorporated in 1935. Increasingly, the *Columbian* documented the social life of these three towns where the workers and their families lived. President Franklin Delano Roosevelt visited twice—once in 1934 and again in 1937—and the *Columbian* celebrated his second visit. The May 20, 1941, issue of the *Columbian* looked back on seven years of hard work and anticipated production of "vast blocks of cheap electric power" and irrigation of 1,200,000 acres in the Columbia Basin—the original, unmet goal of the project.

INCARCERATION OF WASHINGTON JAPANESE

On December 7, 1941, Japanese war planes attacked the U.S. Pacific Fleet docked at Pearl Harbor in Hawaii, sinking eight ships and destroying nearly two hundred aircraft. More than 2,400 servicemen were killed. Within hours, Jack Helms, the regional director of the Office of Civilian Defense, sent this telegram to Washington State's governor, Arthur Langlie, warning against sabotage of the state's infrastructure. Helms did not mention suspicion of Washington residents of Japanese ancestry, but Issei and Nisei—first- and second-generation Japanese—looked like the enemy and became Japanese overnight, instead of Americans. Ethnic Japanese workers at the Weyerhaeuser lumber mill at Snoqualmie Falls wrote an open letter that was published in the *Snoqualmie Valley Record* on December 11, 1941, proclaiming their loyalty. But by May of 1942 the posters "To All Persons of JAPANESE Ancestry" were to be found throughout western Washington State, requiring evacuation by May 16. Eddie Sato was a Seattle teenager who was interned with his family; he sketched the temporary encampment at the Puyallup fairgrounds, known as Camp Harmony. The barracks and the roller coaster stand in ironic commentary on one another. Finally, Dick Kodani wrote home to Miss Groves, his teacher at Bellevue Grade School, from Pinedale Assembly Center in California in May 1942. He was one of about thirteen thousand Washington residents of Japanese descent to be incarcerated during World War II.

A Statement to the Citizens of the Snoqualmie Valley

We, the Japanese Nationals of Snoqualmie Falls, ever since the establishment of our permanent residence in the United States, had always been hoping for the continuation of peaceful relations between this country and Japan.

But, we are now faced with the fact that the United States and Japan are at war. The first news of Japan's unprovoked attack on United States territories was a distinct shock to us as well it may have been to you.

We have been residing in this country for upwards of thirty to forty-five years, in which time we have learned the American way of life. We have lived in peace and happiness among you American people and have been allowed to pursue our regular mode of living. For this we are truly grateful. During the months previous to this present outbreak we have been proud to participate in the National Defense Program. We in this camp have subscribed 100 per cent to the purchase of Defense Bonds. Some have sent sons and brothers to serve in the armed forces of this country. These things we have done proudly and without mental reservation.

Therefore, at this time, we, the Japanese residents of the Snoqualmie Falls Camp, wish to express to you fair minded Americans the fact that we remain loyal and will conform with all the regulations and wartime measures prescribed by the authorities as being necessary to the speedy and successful prosecution of this war till peace once more shall reign in the Pacific.

SNOQUALMIE FALLS JAPANESE NATIONALS

WESTERN DEFENSE COMMAND AND FOURTH ARMY WARTIME CIVIL CONTROL ADMINISTRATION
Presidio of San Francisco, California
May 10, 1942

INSTRUCTIONS TO ALL PERSONS OF JAPANESE ANCESTRY
Living in the Following Area:

All that portion of the County of King, State of Washington, within the boundary beginning at the intersection of Roosevelt Way and East Eighty-fifth Street; thence easterly along East Eighty-fifth Street and East Eighty-fifth Street extended to Lake Washington; thence southerly along the shoreline of Lake Washington to the point at which Yesler Way meets Lake Washington; thence westerly along Yesler Way to Fifteenth Avenue; thence northerly on Fifteenth Avenue to East Madison Street; thence southwesterly along East Madison Street to Fifth Avenue; thence northwesterly along Fifth Avenue to Westlake Avenue; thence northerly along Westlake Avenue to Virginia Street; thence northeasterly along Virginia Street to Fairview Avenue North; thence northerly along Fairview Avenue North to Eastlake Avenue; thence northerly along Eastlake Avenue to Roosevelt Way; thence northerly along Roosevelt Way to the point of beginning.

Pursuant to the provisions of Civilian Exclusion Order No. 57, this Headquarters, dated May 10, 1942, all persons of Japanese ancestry, both alien and non-alien, will be evacuated from the above area by 12 o'clock noon, P. W. T., Saturday, May 16, 1942.

No Japanese person living in the above area will be permitted to change residence after 12 o'clock noon, P. W. T., Sunday, May 10, 1942, without obtaining special permission from the representative of the Commanding General, Northwestern Sector, at the Civil Control Station located at:

Christian Youth Center,
2203 East Madison Street,
Seattle, Washington.

Such permits will only be granted for the purpose of uniting members of a family, or in cases of grave emergency.

The Civil Control Station is equipped to assist the Japanese population affected by this evacuation in the following ways:

1. Give advice and instructions on the evacuation.

2. Provide services with respect to the management, leasing, sale, storage or other disposition of most kinds of property, such as real estate, business and professional equipment, household goods, boats, automobiles and [...]

[...] all Japanese in family groups.

[...] clothing and equipment to their new residence.

[...] served:

[...] bly the head of the family, or the person in whose name most of [...] one, will report to the Civil Control Station to receive further [...] M. and 5:00 P. M. on Monday, May 11, 1942, or between 8:00 [...]

[...] are for the Assembly Center, the following property:

[...] h member of the family;

[...] family;

[...] er of the family.

[...] d and plainly marked with the name of the owner and numbered [...] Civil Control Station. The size and number of packages is limited [...] ual or family group.

[...] ls will be shipped to the Assembly Center.

[...] agencies will provide for the storage, at the sole risk of the owner, [...] as iceboxes, washing machines, pianos and other heavy furniture. [...] accepted for storage if crated, packed and plainly marked with the [...] and address will be used by a given family.

[...] will be furnished transportation to the Assembly Center or will be [...] supervised group. All instructions pertaining to the movement will [...]

[...] between the hours of 8:00 A. M. and 5:00 P. M.,
[...] r between the hours of 8:00 A. M. and 5:00 P. M.,
[...] to receive further instructions.

J. L. DeWITT
Lieutenant General, U. S. Army
Commanding

Postal Telegraph
Mackay Radio *All America Cables*
Commercial Cables *Canadian Pacific Telegraphs*

Form 16 L.

RXRB 125 GOVT=F SANFRANCISCO CALIF 7 500P   Phoned

HON ARTHUR B LANGLIE=

=GOVERNOR'S OFFICE OLYMPIA WASHN=

=OWING SITUATION RESULTING TODAY'S JAPANESE ACTION BELIEVE HIGHLY ESSENTIAL TO DECLARE STATE OF EMERGENCY ALERTING ALL CIVILIAN DEFENSE ORGANIZATIONS AND REQUESTING ALL INDIVIDUAL MEMBERS STAND BY ALSO BELIEVE HIGHLY IMPORTANT EVERY POSSIBLE PRECAUTION BE TAKEN AGAINST SABOTAGE WITH REGARD TO ALL THE VITAL FACILITIES SUCH AS WATER AND POWER SUPPLY,MEANS COMMUNICATION TRANSPORTATION,DEFENSE INDUSTRIES,ETC. SUGGEST THIS INFORMATION BE PASSED TO PROPER LAW ENFORCEMENT OFFICERS REQUESTING SPECIAL GUARDS FOR SUCH FACILITIES. SUGGEST ANY UNORGANIZED COMMUNITIES MAKE FULL USE AMERICAN LEGION. AM SURE THEY WILL COOPERATE FULLY. BELIEVE ESSENTIAL MAXIMUM PRECAUTIONS BE TAKEN UNTIL SITUATION MORE EXACTLY DETERMINED THAN PRESENTLY POSSIBLE. IF SUCH PRECAUTIONS UNNECESSARY CAN BE RELAXED LATER. UNDERSTAND YOU ARE ALREADY TAKING THESE PRECAUTIONS BUT HAVE SENT WIRE IN CASE SOME WERE OVERLOOKED=

=JACK H HELMS

ACTING REGIONAL DIRECTOR US OFFICE CIVILIAN DEFENSE.(00)

E-33-Apt. 5
Pinedale, Calf.
May 25, 1942

Dear Miss Groves,

I arrived here May 20, 1942 after a very nice train ride. The soldiers and porters were very nice and polite Pinedale is very pretty. We saw our first orange tree. It is very hot here but I am getting used to it. the day we came here we had to boil the water before we drank it. I have lots of fun with other boys but I wish I was back home. I hope you have a nice picnic! Please write to me

very truly,
Dick Kodani

e-3-4 1st Strat
Pinedale assembly center
Pinedale, Calif.

Forward

Miss P. Groves
527-31st Ave. So
Bellevue Grade School
Bellevue Washington
Seattle, Washington

FRESNO
MAY 29
4 PM
1942
CALIF.

UNITED STATES
POSTAGE
3 CENTS

WARTIME HOME FRONT

Washington State was mobilized on the World War II home front, from the fields and orchards to the shipyards and factories. Discipline and self-sacrifice were key to winning the war. The certificate above commended the men and women employed by Washington State for pledging at least ten percent of their pay to the purchase of war bonds. Everyone was encouraged to conserve scarce materials for the war effort: silk, rubber, and tea had disappeared; gasoline and liquor were both in short supply; and food was rationed. Elizabeth Gustison's War Ration Book and its coupons for sugar, meat, and other essentials, are shown above.

The federal government published dozens of brochures and posters in an effort to help Americans plant victory gardens and to learn to do more with less. To the right, familiar figures from 1940s comic strips exhorted Americans to "Eat Right to Work and Win," encouraging a fruit juice bar in the basement and a big garden of vegetables for home harvest and canning. The 1943 brochure *Root Vegetables in Wartime Meals* urged the use of not just potatoes but other filling, carbohydrate-rich turnips, beets, and other root vegetables in wartime menu planning.

EAT RIGHT
TO WORK AND WIN

HERE'S A CHANCT TO KNOW YORE VITTLES!! TIMES A WASTIN', FOLKS!!

Contributed by Swift & Company to America's All-Out War Effort through the National Nutrition Program.

OFFICE OF DEFENSE HEALTH AND WELFARE SERVICES

Comic characters donated by King Features Syndicate.

Root Vegetables in Wartime Meals

U.S. DEPARTMENT OF AGRICULTURE

AWI-39

Toots and Casper . . . . . by Jimmy Murphy

CASPER, I WISH YOU'D GIVE UP THE IDEA OF HAVING A BAR IN THE RECREATION ROOM!

YEAH, BUT WAIT'LL YOU SEE IT!

SOME CLASS, EH?

they go on eating right. They'll have more fun every year of their lives. They'll have the high courage it takes to meet our war problems today, and the clear heads and strong hearts to remake a war-torn world. *They'll have what it takes.*

Look at the men in our new Army. Not all of them got the kind of care as babies that we've just described. And do you remember how they looked when they first

---

Thimble Theater . . . . Starring Popeye

BLOW ME DOWN! AN' HERE I BIN CONFININ' MESELF TO SPINACH!

Do it selfishly at first, if you like; because you want your family to be happy and successful; because they can't be either happy or on their toes if they aren't stoked with the right kind of food fuel. Do it, knowing that it's your job and that it will take more skill than perhaps you've ever before devoted to the job of cooking. Do it for the fun of watching them perk up and

---

Tillie the Toiler . . . . . by Russ Westover

WHAT WE NEED ARE MORE VEGETABLES AND FRUITS—I JUST LOVE TO WORK IN THE GARDEN

YEAH, DON'T SHE, THOUGH!

lowering of vitality and capacity to work which comes from failure to eat the right variety of food.

Does this sound like the medicine man's Chamber of Horrors? Well, keep it in mind, but don't brood over it. For if your family eats the basic foods you can laugh in the teeth of this man-made nightmare.

What, specifically, to do?

Four things, easy to remember, easy to do, if you get the habit.

The first step is to PLAN YOUR MEALS before you go to market. You are going to have some kind of meat or fish or poultry, some vegetables, some cereals and bread, eggs, milk, butter, fruit, and so on. You can decide which ones to buy when you get to the store and see what is fresh and good and plentiful.

Step number two is to make sure that your family gets some of these foods *every day:*

Milk For a growing child, ¾ to 1 quart every day. For other family members, 1 pint or more.

Tomatoes, oranges, grapefruit, green cabbage, raw salad greens One or more servings.

SERVE VICTORY MEALS

PAGE 10

The Phantom . . by Lee Falk and Ray Moore

FRIED MUSH AND EGGS—UM—THAT SMELLS GOOD!

SURE, DIANA, THE DAY ALWAYS STARTS RIGHT, AFTER A GOOD BREAKFAST OF CEREAL, EGGS, BACON, BREAD---

Leafy, green, or yellow vegetables—One or more servings for each person.

Other vegetables, fruit—Two or more servings.

Eggs—One egg every day, or at least 3 each week.

Meat, poultry, fish—At least 1 serving a day.

Cereals and bread—At least 2 servings of whole-grain products or "enriched" bread—or cereals restored to whole-grain value.

Fats—Serve ½ to 1 pound to each person each week.

Sweets—Use sugar and other sweets in moderation.

Water—Six or more glasses each day.

VITAMINS are substances which are found in every food and are necessary to growth and general good health. Without them the minerals, proteins, carbohydrates, and fats are not properly used in the body. Vegetables, fruits, milk, meat, fish, whole wheat or enriched bread, and eggs are excellent sources of vitamins.

IN PLANNING YOUR MEALS USE CHART ON PAGES 8 AND 9

Step number three is PROPER COOKING. Don't use too much water in cooking foods. When you cook with water, it is very easy to cook the vitamins right out of the foods. Always *save the water* in which foods are cooked. Don't throw it down the sink.

PAGE

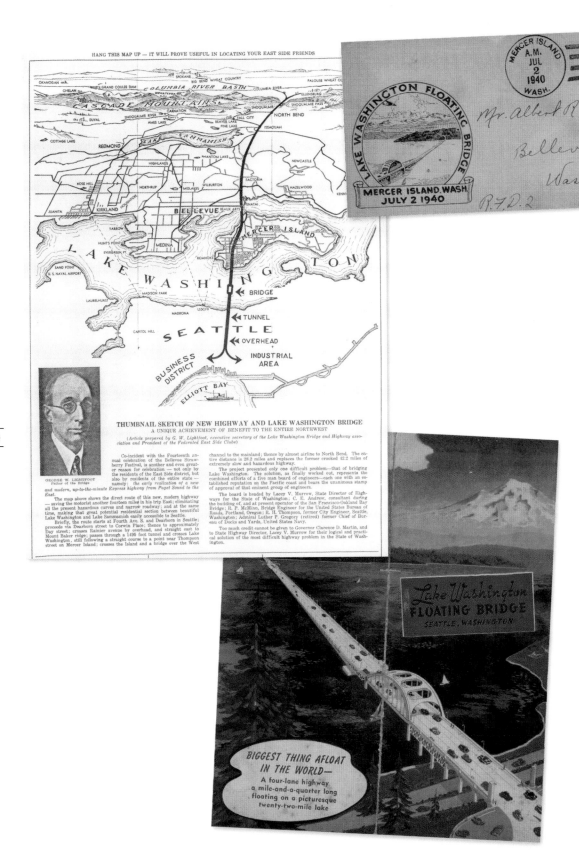

THUMBNAIL SKETCH OF NEW HIGHWAY AND LAKE WASHINGTON BRIDGE
A UNIQUE ACHIEVEMENT OF BENEFIT TO THE ENTIRE NORTHWEST
(Article prepared by G. W. Lightfoot, executive secretary of the Lake Washington Bridge and Highway association and President of the Federated East Side Clubs)

GEORGE W. LIGHTFOOT
Father of the Bridge

BIGGEST THING AFLOAT
IN THE WORLD—
A four-lane highway
a mile-and-a-quarter long
floating on a picturesque
twenty-two-mile lake

Lake Washington
FLOATING BRIDGE
SEATTLE, WASHINGTON

BRIDGE TO THE FUTURE

On July 2, 1940, the Lacey V. Murrow Memorial Bridge opened to traffic. The floating bridge offered cheap and easy transit across Lake Washington, in addition to the ferries that crossed from Madison Park to Kirkland. George Lightfoot became known as the "father of the bridge," for his indefatigable, decade-long advocacy. His article and the accompanying map demonstrate the benefits of the bridge and its direct route, which opened a new residential district between Lake Washington and Lake Sammamish and connected Seattle more readily to Eastern Washington. The opening day ceremonies program showed the bridge crossing the beautiful lake with picturesque Mount Rainier in the distance, and boasted of the "Biggest Thing Afloat in the World." A tiny handful of cars crossed the bridge in this illustration—perhaps many preferred a drive around the lake to paying the twenty-five cent toll. Boosters promised that one day soon, the bridge might handle as many as 2,800 cars per day! Or 116 cars per hour! Jokes aside, the first Lake Washington Floating Bridge truly led to the future. After the war the GI Bill offered veterans the opportunity to buy a new home, no money down, with a government-insured low interest loan; GI Bill residential subdivisions like Eastgate and Lake Hills flourished along the I-90 corridor. In 1950 the last ferry crossed Lake Washington, and in 1953 Bellevue was incorporated. Today the bridge has nearly doubled in width, and about 140,000 vehicles cross it each day.

The following text appears within the illustration (newspaper front page):

On the Ways

PUBLISHED BY THE LAKE WASHINGTON SHIPYARDS · HOUGHTON, WASHINGTON
DECEMBER 24, 1942   VOLUME 1, NUMBER 30

CHRISTMAS, this year, is unlike any in the history of the world. Not a spot on earth is free from the shadow of war, destruction and chaos. Treasured ideas and philosophies of life in all countries are being dashed to pieces.

Christmas is all things to all men. To some the Holiday will be devoted to personal pleasures, cheer and good food. To lonely Marines standing guard on tiny atolls in the South Pacific, it will be a day of vigil and thoughts of home. The night watchers on the coast of England will look to the East, and to sensitive souls the dead will plead "let this be the last of human carnage."

We in America have cause to be deeply thankful. Our homes are intact. No bombs have blown our families to bits. As a nation we are achieving perspective in this battle for the Rights of Man, and our efforts to produce the instruments of war are more resultful day by day.

To us at LWS, Christmas 1942 has deep significance. The ships we are building are of primary importance in winning the war. All of us pause on this day of Christianity to rededicate our ideals, our faith in our way of life, our faith in God, and renew our pledge to work and fight for victory—to end aggression and tyranny, so that Light and Peace can return to the world.

SANTA GOES TO WAR

The Lake Washington Shipyards in Houghton, south of Kirkland, mobilized on the wartime home front to produce seaplane tenders and antisubmarine net tenders for the U.S. Navy. This tiny prewar shipyard had employed about three hundred men to build fishing vessels, yachts, and oceanographic survey ships. But by Christmas Eve 1942 the shipyard was on its way to its wartime-high employment of 8,500 men and women working three shifts around the clock. The Lake Washington Shipyards newspaper, *On the Ways*, encouraged the yard's welders, boilermakers, machinists, electricians, sheet-metal workers, and shipfitters to work quickly and well, but safely, too. Newcomers to the shipyard—Okies and Arkies, African Americans and women—were warned to be doubly careful. But *On the Ways* also provided constant reminders of what the war was all about. Here Santa Claus stands east of the Cascade Mountains, looking down at Lake Washington Shipyards on the lakefront of Yarrow Bay. Dressed in Christmas colors, he has exchanged his cap for a hardhat and sports an identification badge on his coveralls—his gift is a warship. In fact, the star-spangled Christmas stocking is stuffed with armaments.

Hanford, Washington 1943-1945

Numbers of employees quartered in barracks - 40,000
Numbers of employees quartered in trailer camps - 8,000
$3,500,000.00 worth of meal tickets in 8 months through payroll deductions
Meal tickets sold for cash, not included in above
Four million lunch boxes sold from July, 1943 to October, 1944
Eight mess halls. 2,700 in each mess hall at each setting is the capacity, usually 3 settings.
272,000 lbs. of processed meat, ready for oven or grill, used in one week
5,000 lbs. of sausage used for one breakfast
2,500 lbs. of pot roast for one meal
18,000 pork chops for one meal for 1 mess hall (8 mess halls-144,000 pork chops)
15 tons of potatoes for one mess hall each day (8 mess halls-120 tons)
5,000 heads of lettuce for each meal for 1 mess hall (8 mess halls-40,000 heads)
1,200 lbs. of onions for one meal for one mess hall (8 mess halls-9,600 lbs.)
900 full pies for one meal for one mess hall (8 mess halls-7,200 pies)
1,000 lbs. of coffee for one day for one mess hall (8 mess halls-8,000 lbs.)
30,000 doughnuts for one day
2,200 loaves of bread used each day for sandwiches not counting bread on tables
200 lbs. of butter for one day for sandwiches used on packing lunches
Sandwich machine makes 360 sandwiches per hour (3 machines in operation)
11,000 lbs. of Swiss steak for one meal for all mess halls
250,000 lbs. of meat used for all mess halls for one week
10,000 newspapers sold each day by recreation halls
16,000 packages of cigarettes sold each day
12,000 gallons of beer consumed each week (13 carloads)
2,000 keys for barracks lost each month by employees
Dishes for mess halls are first soaked in soap solution, then racked and passed through water jets at high pressure of 120 degrees, then through live steam
Menus are prepared 60 days in advance
Grades of meat used - choice, good, and comercial
All meals are planned for balanced diet (for manual labor)
The only time fried eggs can be served is Sunday morning because meals are served over a longer period of time
6,500 eggs are used for Sunday breakfast
700 cases of Coke per day
600 gallons of ice cream per day
It would take 250 good cows to supply the milk for one breakfast
1,785,000 sheets washed - if these were tied together, they would reach from Hanford to New York City
1,000,000 meal ticket cards on file (active and inactive)
Automatic doughnut machine makes 18,000 per hour
12,000 turkeys for Thanksgiving (22 tons of turkey - 12 tons of ham)
Hanford is the largest voting precinct in the U.S.
Hanford has the largest general delivery post office in the world

c. Climate

The mean temperature, based on recordings over a ten-year period, range from a maximum of 75° F. to a minimum of 11° F. above zero. Average annual precipitation at Hanford is recorded at 5.93 inches. Available weather reports indicate a maximum frost depth of 18 inches.

d. Agriculture

At the commencement of land acquisition approximately 1,500 inhabitants within the Site Area were engaged in either ranching or farming. In all 13,487 acres were under dry farming, and 18,000 acres lay within irrigation districts, though not more than 6,000 acres were actually irrigated. Irrigated tracts were devoted to growing a variety of products, mainly; cherries, apricots, peaches, prunes, pears, apples, grapes, asparagus, and potatoes. A limited amount of grain and some alfalfa was produced. It was estimated by the Federal Land Bank that the total value of all crops raised in the Richland and Priest Rapids Irrigation Districts during 1942 was approximately $2,119,250.00.

Prior to the introduction of irrigation in 1908, the area was utilized exclusively for grazing. All but three per cent of the acreage within the boundaries of the Plant Site was suitable for this purpose. The Department of Agriculture had estimated that 120 acres of this land was required to support five sheep for five and one-half months per year. This estimate was indicative of the inferior quality of the soil. Range land was used primarily for sheep during the spring and winter seasons.

COMPLETION REPORT

HANFORD ENGINEER WORKS

PART I

A. Description of Site

1. Geographic Location

The Hanford Engineer Works is located in parts of Grant, Franklin, Benton and Yakima Counties in the south central section of the State of Washington. The Plant Site is bounded on the north and east by the Columbia River and on the west by the Rattlesnake Hills and the Yakima Range. The westernmost boundary of the Site is thirty-four air-line miles east of Yakima, Washington, a city of 28,840 population; and the southeast corner, 49 air-line miles northwest of Walla Walla, Washington, a city of 18,109. Other cities, towns, and villages in the immediate vicinity of the Project are as follows:

Name	Distance	Population
Kennewick	33.4 miles	1,918
Pasco	36.7 miles	8,500
Benton City	24.2 miles	300
Grandview	48.8 miles	1,876
Sunnyside	56.8 miles	3,500
Prosser	41.1 miles	2,250
Connell	33.0 miles	450

Note: These distances are road miles to Hanford, which was the temporary housing center for the construction of the Plant.

4. Electricity

Operating power used and transmitted by the Project's electrical systems is purchased from the Bonneville Power Administration as per agreement executed on February 26, 1944, by the Bonneville Power Administration and the United States Government. Permanent electric power required for the operation of the 100 and 200 Process Areas is supplied directly from the 230 KV transmission system of the Bonneville Power Administration through its Midway Substation, which has for its immediate feeders Grand Coulee and Bonneville Hydro-Electric Plants. Power for the 300, 700, and 1100 Areas is obtained from the 115 KV Midway-Walla Walla tie-line of Bonneville Power Administration, from which delivery is made through the former Pacific Power and Light Company's Substation at Hanford. These areas can be supplied in emergency through Pacific Power and Light Company's Substation at Pasco. At these substations the voltage is reduced to 66 KV before final delivery to the above areas over former existing transmission lines of the Pacific Power and Light Company. All transmission lines, properties, and appurtenances of the Pacific Power and Light Company within the Project's boundaries were acquired by the Government.

2. The Plant

The Hanford Engineer Works, a plant for the manufacture of a classified end product is composed primarily of seven separate process areas, five service areas, and one village made up of residences plus attendant commercial and service structures.

3. Water Supply

Because of the nature of process manufacturing, and the arid condition in the Richland Village Housing Area, large quantities of water were required for the Project. Three different sources and methods were employed to develop an adequate water supply.

a. The water supply for the 100 and 200 Process Areas is taken directly from the Columbia River by means of three River Pump House Buildings, one located in each of the 100 Areas. An export water system composed of reinforced concrete pipe inter-connects the pumping plants in each area and supplies raw water to the 200-E and 200-W Areas. Each river pumping plant is designed to provide 20,000 GPM above its area requirements, whereby an adequate water supply can be maintained in case one of the pump houses in the 100 Areas is temporarily shut down. A large reinforced concrete reservoir is provided in each area as an additional safety factor. The capacity of each reservoir is:

Area	Raw Water Reservoir Capacity
100-B	25,000,000 gallons
100-D	25,000,000 gallons
100-F	25,000,000 gallons
200-E	3,000,000 gallons
200-W	3,000,000 gallons

WASHINGTON'S MANHATTAN PROJECT

Before World War II, White Bluffs and Hanford were small, sleepy farming communities in central Washington, clearly visible on the 1934 Columbia Basin Project map. Then, in 1943, the Manhattan Project came to town, its engineers hunting for a site to build a secret manufacturing plant. They required a remote and isolated place; a supply of clean, cool water; a sparse population; and abundant electric power—and they found all that just west of Richland, Washington. Fifteen hundred local residents were relocated from Hanford and White Bluffs, and construction began in March 1943. The Hanford Engineer Works was home to the B Reactor, the first full-scale plutonium production reactor in the world. The B Reactor produced its first plutonium November 6, 1944, and manufactured the plutonium used in the atomic bomb detonated over Nagasaki, Japan. Above are excerpts from the *Completion Report*, 1945, of the Hanford Engineer Works, ranging across Hanford's production to a snapshot of life for the fifty thousand workers and their families.

MARKETING POSTWAR SEATTLE

The Seattle Chamber of Commerce, anticipating the end of the war, published this 1944 pamphlet to boost the city's postwar position on the Pacific Rim. Distinguishing the "outer harbor" of Elliott Bay from the "inner harbor" of the freshwater Lakes Union and Washington, the chamber made the case for waterborne shipping. However, Seattle-Tacoma International Airport was under construction in 1944, and the chamber also anticipated its postwar use for airborne passengers and freight. During the war, the pamphlet continued, Seattle's factories had produced $3.5 billion in war matériel, from ships and planes to Sherman tanks. These factories, streamlined for war, would be transformed to peacetime uses in the city poised to take advantage of its manufacturing and transportation primacy on Puget Sound.

DICK DONNELL PARODIES HANFORD, 1946

Fifty thousand men and women worked at the top secret Hanford Engineer Works during World War II, and only the smallest handful of them knew its purpose. Housing for the scientists, engineers, and workers was hastily constructed but instant communities sprang up to share the hard work and the harsh way of life. When the typical winds swept through, penetrating every wall and depositing sand on every tabletop, the hardy joked that they were "termination winds," as the less hardy simply disappeared. On August 6, 1945, the *Richland Villager* headline ran "It's Atomic Bombs—President Truman Releases Secret of Hanford Product," ending the mystery. August 6 was the day an atomic bomb was dropped on Hiroshima, and three days before one incorporating Hanford plutonium would be dropped on Nagasaki. Hanford worker Dick Donnell cartooned for the *Villager*; two of his cartoons were scanned from the microfilmed *Villager* and reproduced here. Donnell created "Dupus Boomer," the eponymous DuPont employee whose misadventures brought smiles to readers. First Donnell joked about atomic security, as a zealous guard vacuumed Dupus for a missing atom, published July 18, 1946, and he sketched a telling cartoon of a typical worker's prefab house and its very hot, very flat roof, published July 25, 1946. As the hot war segued to the Cold War, and DuPont to General Electric, work at Hanford carried on and everyday life continued in the atomic boomtowns of Hanford and Richland.

"ALL I KNOW SIR, IS THAT AN ATOM APPEARS TO BE MISSING."

"NICE OF THEM TO LOAN US A LADDER UNTIL THEY CAN FIX THE STOVE."

PAPER DOLLS

Not all archival material is documents, photographs, and maps. This World War II era paper doll set was played with by starstruck little girls in the home of Seattle businessman Joshua Green. This selection shows only about one-quarter of the clothing, hats, handbags, and other accessories in the set, all in wonderful condition. The doll represented Shirley Temple, the great Depression era child star, as a teenager on the wartime home front. World War II significantly influenced the clothing shown here, including the military-style suit and dress and the patriotic American flag pin on the suit. Nevertheless, Temple held a movie fan magazine in her left hand, showing that ordinary life went on even in a world at war.

How to Spot a Communist

and

Slick Tricks of the Commies

By

KARL BAARSLAG

Reprints of a series of articles appearing in the January and February, 1947, issues of The American Legion Magazine.

☆

To fulfill a great demand for copies of this series of articles, this Reprint has been made by

National Americanism Commission
THE AMERICAN LEGION
777 N. Meridian Street
Indianapolis 6, Indiana

First Report

Un-American Activities

in

Washington State

1948

Report of the Joint Legislative Fact-Finding
Committee on Un-American Activities

Mr. Canwell: To conclude in any way that people who joined the Communist fronts, or were deceived, or hoodwinked or succumbed to their propaganda are ipso facto Communists would be silly. That isn't what the fronts are all about. They were to influence and recruit people into general socialist activity. They were not, and should not, automatically be considered to be Communists. It would be like saying that just because somebody votes for Brock Adams that they believe in drugging and raping little girls. That isn't the way it works.

People have reasons for supporting these fronts, many of them sound very good. With a little persuasion by very knowledgeable, persuasive persons, they go along. There was just an enormous amount of that during the New Deal period. I think of my contact here in Spokane, Mrs. Webster. She went along with the Communist Party because she thought that they were for the workingman per se, and believed it. But she was only a Communist for a limited time.

In saying that, I should differentiate between these professors who led out in the front movement—that's an entirely different thing. The leadership is an entirely different thing than the followers. The leadership has to provide the effort, the bait, and they fish in troubled waters. The Communists always do. But to exonerate anybody who was prominent in say twelve or fifteen of these major Communist fronts and to say that he just wasn't a Communist—he named himself a Communist by so doing. It isn't incumbent on every investigator and every government agent to come up with documentary proof on people who are in the Communist Party. It's desirable when you can, but it's often impossible. It doesn't mean that the person isn't guilty.

iv *Preface*

1. Communists in the State of Washington operate under, and undeviatingly follow, policies laid down for them by the Soviet government.

2. These policies are promulgated on a nation-wide basis and that the activities of Communists in the State of Washington are coordinated with Communist activities in the other states of the union.

3. The dovetailed nation-wide program is designed to create distrust of their form of government in the minds and hearts of the American people; create unrest and civil strife, and impede the normal processes of state and national government, all to the end of weakening and ultimately destroying the United States as a constitutional republic and thereby facilitating the avowed Soviet purpose of substituting here a totalitarian dictatorship.

Fantastic as this may appear to the uninitiate and the naive, the testimony produced at the public hearings clearly brings into view the extreme danger of the Soviet directed Communist conspiracy to the peace and security of the people of the State of Washington and the United States.

The Committee wishes to lay special emphasis on the fact that its testimony and documentary evidence were made possible by the tireless and devoted labor of a highly specialized staff of investigators, all of whom have had years of training in the investigative field in various branches of the Federal government.

ALBERT F. CANWELL, *Chairman*

HUNTING FOR COMMUNISTS

At the end of World War II, the United States was preeminent among the Allies and held the monopoly on atomic technology. But as the Iron Curtain was drawn over much of Eastern Europe and the Union of Soviet Socialist Republics detonated its first atomic weapon in 1949, the Cold War began. The U.S. identified the Soviet Union as its principal enemy, the exporter of the ideology of Communism throughout the world. Washington had been the butt of a 1936 joke by Postmaster General James Farley, that there were forty-seven states in the United States, and the Soviet of Washington. By 1947 the joke seemed far less funny, and the state legislature authorized the Joint Legislative Fact-Finding Committee on Un-American Activities in Washington, chaired by freshman representative Albert Canwell of Spokane. The Canwell Committee, as it came to be known, convened two hearings in 1948 to investigate Communist Party influence in labor unions, pension organizations, and among university faculty. Though the committee's express intent was to frame legislation, the hearings actually became a kangaroo court in which a parade of witnesses accused men and women of Communist convictions, their testimony reported by blaring headlines in daily newspapers. Here you see a 1947 American Legion brochure, *How to Spot a Communist*, as well as the Canwell Committee's three conclusions published in *First Report: Un-American Activities in Washington State, 1948*. In 1997, the Washington State Oral History program interviewed Canwell, and here is an excerpt from that transcript.

Travel is a pleasure aboard ship

ALASKANS look forward to trips outside on steamers of THE ALASKA LINE. Every voyage is like "old home week" because you know you will meet many of your friends during the cruise. Newcomers join in the activities, too. The pleasant pace of life aboard ship promotes friendliness and enjoyable sociability.

There is also the pleasure of good food and comfortable accommodations . . . and the convenience of regular schedules.

Oldtimers and cheechakos alike prefer travel on Alaska Line steamers. When it's travel time, take THE ALASKA LINE.

ALASKA STEAMSHIP COMPANY
Serving All Alaska

WATER HIGHWAY TO ALASKA

During World War II the Alaska Steamship Company's ships were federalized. Afterward the company continued to offer passenger service between Alaska ports and Seattle, and also moved more strongly into containerized shipping. This advertisement spoke to the passenger service, as Alaskans—whether old-timers or newcomer "cheechakos"—"look[ed] forward to trips outside." These voyages "outside" ended at Seattle, known as Alaska's living room and Alaska's pantry in those years, where Alaskans could enjoy the delights of a big city, from shopping for fashionable clothes to a visit to the Seattle Art Museum. Published in 1949, this ad ran in nearly every Alaska magazine and daily newspaper. The Alaska Steamship Company discontinued passenger service in 1954, ending an era that had begun in 1894.

YAKIMA FIELD LABOR

Here a group of articles from the *Goodfruit Grower*, 1946–48, explores life in Eastern Washington orchards just after World War II. In an article concerned with housing for migrant workers, a spokesman noted the pressing need for small cabins to house pickers and their families, who had numbered eighty thousand the previous harvest season. Mentioned in the *Goodfruit Grower's* article, Young's Lumber Company, in Yakima, soon advertised ready-built cabins for use by farm laborers. Berry's Yakima Tent and Awning Company bought advertising space for picking bags, machine stitched and leather bound, specially designed with a "chute bottom" to prevent fruit bruising. The Rainier Printing Company, also in Yakima, advertised picker's tickets, to be punched as fruit was picked. Sears' Lumber Company issued a postcard that advertised tree props to support heavily fruited branches. Together, these documents describe the hard labor of harvesting Washington fruit, and the spartan living conditions of laboring families, mostly Chicano, who worked the orchards.

LAKE CHELAN APPLES

On August 25, 1910, the *Chelan Leader* newspaper editorialized that "extensive adoption by shippers of apple box labels" would help publicize area apples and boost their sales. "When a person in the East or middle West goes into a fruit store to buy apples," continued the editor, "his eye rests on great numbers of boxes" pasted with attractive labels. Unlike Chelan growers, he went on, Wenatchee and Yakima growers had commissioned printing houses to design such labels, "depicting orchards nesting in mountain valleys and numerous other attractive scenes." Here, in the late 1940s, is the proof of that wise advice to Chelan-area orchardists: a beautiful label for a bushel of apples, trumpeting the orchards of Lake Chelan and featuring an evocative painting of the lake and its surrounding mountains. Washington State growers commissioned hundreds of such labels, beautifully designed and colored by unknown, unsung commercial artists.

EL RANCHITO, 1954

El Ranchito opened in Zillah in the Yakima Valley in about 1953 and became a center for Chicano families throughout Eastern Washington. Cesar Chavez and many other well-known men and women made it a point to visit El Ranchito. Decorated with hundreds of piñatas and colorful streamers, "The Little Ranch" was widely considered the best Mexican restaurant in eastern Washington, and also operated a tortilla factory and a grocery store specializing in Mexican foods. In 1997 the tortilla business was sold to Mission Foods, and the restaurant closed in 2007.

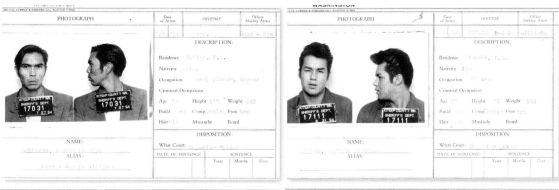

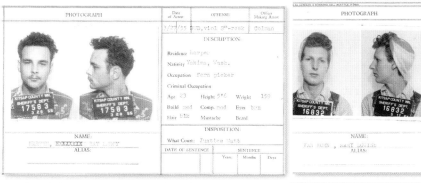

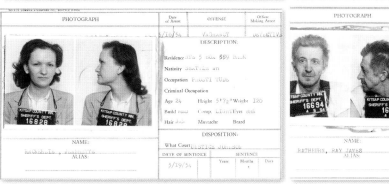

BOOKING PHOTOS

These booking shots were taken in the Kitsap County sheriff's office in 1954. Spurred by naval construction projects during World War II and then the Korean War, the Puget Sound Naval Shipyard brought workers and sailors from throughout the United States to Bremerton. Opportunities in local woods and fields brought agricultural laborers from British Columbia, Oregon, and Washington. Some of them got into trouble, and their solemn faces gaze at the camera and at us across more than a half century—accused of vagrancy; prostitution; sodomy; drunk driving; burglary; selling beer to minors; leaving the *U.S.S. Prairie* without official leave; or the cryptic infraction "TMVWOOP B-W/A," which *may* mean "Taking Motor Vehicle With Out Owner's Permission Bench-Warrant Arrest," but may have just as much to do with being an Indian from out of town. Some cases went to court, some were under Navy jurisdiction.

PROTEST BROCHURE

In about 1948 this brochure was published on behalf of the citizens of Clallam, Grays Harbor, and Jefferson counties who believed that Olympic National Park was too large and should be restricted to the scenic high peaks. Requesting that the U.S. Congress "Investigate, Please!" this brochure asserted that all Olympic Peninsula residents were proud of the national park, but then set out arguments to demonstrate that "more land than [was] needed" had been taken for the park and should be returned to the jurisdiction of the U.S. Forest Service. These prime timberlands were "locked up" in Olympic National Park and removed from productive use, creating economic hardship that wouldn't be tolerated if it were cornfields in Iowa or cotton fields in the South. Opponents also argued that national park policies prohibiting the removal of deadfall had created fire hazards that endangered the entire peninsula. The brochure claimed that releasing land from the park would create more lowland recreational opportunities, because then-current logging techniques would not create a desert of clear-cuts. Olympic National Park was not reduced in size, but this protest has left us a well-argued and carefully designed document.

ＡＥＲＯＣＡＲ

"The Flying Automobile"

THE CAR
WITH THE BUILT-IN FREEWAY

AEROCAR is the all-purpose vehicle the traveling public has dreamed of. The powerful little coupe with its fluid drive and unencumbered by wings is ideal for driving in traffic—fast on the get-away and easy to park—a full fledged automobile in every respect. AEROCARS comply with all highway vehicle codes.

As an airplane, the AEROCAR is a roomy, fast means of travel above the snarls of highways, crossing mountains and rivers as though they didn't exist. If bad weather makes flying impractical, you merely land at the nearest airport, fold the wings and they **become a trailer**. With your trailer in tow, you can then continue on to your destination by highway. It is not necessary to leave the wings at the airport and then have to return for them. The change-over requires no more effort than changing a tire and can be done by one person.

The entire AEROCAR may be kept at your home in your own garage, eliminating hangar rent and inconvenience. If your trip does not require flying, the AEROCAR is always ready for instant use, day and night, just like any conventional automobile. When you desire to fly, you can tow the flight unit to the nearest airport, spread the wings, and the unlimited highways of the air are yours.

AEROCARS have been proven by years of test and use. They have been driven thousands of miles in city and highway traffic. The trailers have been towed under all kinds of weather conditions, and AEROCARS have amassed many thousands of hours of flight experience and perform like any other modern light plane of similar weight and power. They are stable, easy to fly, and exceptionally easy to land. AEROCARS are fully approved by the C.A.A. (Type Cert. No. 4A16).

AEROCARS are **now available** in limited production. Public acceptance and the availability of financing will determine how quickly mass production will enable us to deliver AEROCARS at our goal price of **LESS THAN $10,000.00.**

PERFORMANCE

Top Speed	Over 110 MPH
Cruising Speed	Over 100 MPH
Rate of Climb (1st Min @ full load)	Over 550 FPM
Service Ceiling @ full load	Over 12,000 Ft.
Cruise Range	Over 300 Miles
Landing Speed	50 MPH
Landing Run (with normal braking)	300 Ft.
Take-off Run	650 Ft.
Distance to Clear 50 ft. Obstacle	1225 Ft.
Designed Road Speed (Engine red line)	67 MPH
Road Range	Over 400 Miles
Fuel Consumption (Cruising)	8 GPH
Road Fuel Consumption	18 MPG
Time to Change from Plane to Car	Five Min.

SPECIFICATIONS

Wing Span	34 Ft.
Wing Area	190 Sq. Ft.
Wing Loading	11-lb/Sq. Ft.
Power Loading	14.7-lb/HP
Car Empty Weight	1100 Lbs.
Trailer Weight	400 Lbs.
Design Useful Load	600 Lbs.
Allowed Baggage Weight	100 Lbs.
Pilot and Passenger Weight	340 Lbs.
Fuel Weight (24 Gals.)	144 Lbs.
Maximum Gross Weight	2100 Lbs.
Auto Road Tread	5'2"
Auto Wheel Base	6'8"
Trailer Wheel Tread	5'2"
Car-Trailer Length	26'
Baggage Space	14 Cu. Ft.
Wheel and Tire Size	4.50x12
Engine—LYCOMING O-320 (derated)	143 HP
Trailer Wheel Size	10x3.50x4
Seat Width	44"
Trailer Width	96"
Trailer Length	15'
Car Ground Clearance	12"
Height (Aircraft)	7'6"
Height (Car)	5'4"
Height (Trailer)	8'

Manufactured by AEROCAR, Inc., Longview, Wash.

ABOVE GRIDLOCK

After World War II, Moulton "Molt" Taylor returned home to Longview from engineering duty in the U.S. Navy, filled with ideas and ambition. In 1947, he successfully invited fifty investors in the Longview area to each contribute $1000 to his startup for the development and production of a "roadable" aircraft—a flying automobile. The first official flight of the Aerocar took place on December 8, 1949, at Toledo, Washington. This advertisement was printed in the mid-1950s and fully described Molt Taylor's "Car With the Built-In Freeway." If the Aerocar driver wished to avoid gridlock, he simply transformed the vehicle into an airplane and flew above the highways; if he wished to drive, the wings and tail formed a trailer behind the vehicle. It was that simple. Molt Taylor was a tireless promoter, appearing on the TV show *I've Got a Secret* and persuading actor Bob Cummings to purchase an Aerocar. But it proved impossible to find an industrial partner with the capital to build Aerocars in mass production and bring the price down. Today the Museum of Flight in Seattle has an Aerocar on display.

SEW PATIO FASHIONS, AT HOME

By the 1950s World War II's Rosie the Riveter was married and living in a suburban residential sub-division, raising kids, baking cookies, and hosting barbecues. Many Washington State women owned sewing machines and made clothing for their children and for themselves. This Simplicity pattern from 1956 is a colorful reminder of the suburban housewife's busy lifestyle, as she could easily switch from these casual capri pants to a more formal look by buttoning on a simple skirt. Simplicity patterns were sized and then printed onto large paper tracing sheets, which the consumer cut out and pinned to fabric she had chosen, cutting out the pieces to be sewn together. The pattern cost fifty cents, and fabric to make the pants and skirt cost about one dollar and fifty cents—a very inexpensive outfit if all went well for the amateur seamstress.

TWIN TEEPEES MENU

Here we see the cover and interior of the Twin T-P's menu, printed in about 1955. Earlier we looked at the Real Property Record Card for the Twin Teepees restaurant, and it's interesting to compare the photographs with the artist's rendering of the T-P's rustic themes on this menu's cover. The restaurant was comprised of two teepee-style two-story buildings, each with a gas-powered fireplace, joined by a passage with an almost art deco public doorway. The menu pointed out that the restaurant was "different"; that diners would enjoy eating by the "campfire's glow"; and proudly explained that not only was all food selection, preparation, and service under "Homer's" direction, Homer also offered a heart-stopping dessert special and would cheerfully accept all suggestions "for the betterment of our ideals." Washington State's online encyclopedia of history, HistoryLink.org, offers two fine articles on the history of Twin Teepees, through its much-lamented demolition in 2001. The Twin Teepees was a fun place to eat, and a true Seattle original.

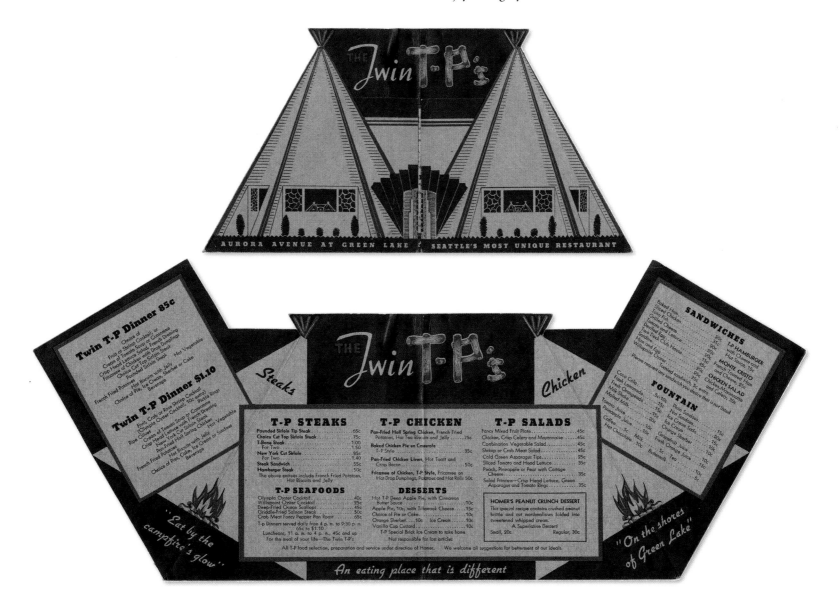

LAKE WASHINGTON CRISIS

It was not a simple thing to make regional treatment of sewage and wastewater a family issue, but this political poster encouraging a "yes" vote for Metro did so. It was the perfect image at the perfect time, perfectly attuned to the sensibilities of 1950s suburban and city voters. The poster declared an EMERGENCY! over an image of five vulnerable children unable to swim because of FILTHY WATERS. Summertime beach closures on Lake Washington were commonplace as untreated sewage poured into the lake from the towns around its shoreline. Inspired by visionary Jim Ellis, a group of citizens became convinced that such a shared problem could only be solved by formation of a metropolitan municipal corporation, to unite the Seattle-King County region. In the spring of 1958, a measure to establish the Municipality of Metropolitan Seattle (Metro) with sweeping responsibilities was placed before the voters, approved in Seattle but voted down in the suburbs. On September 9, 1958, the creation of Metro was once again on the ballot, this time focused only on water pollution, the most compelling issue, and the initiative won a resounding victory throughout the region. This poster was a crucial document in that campaign, appealing to the voter's heart and mind: between the little girl in her white swimsuit to the boy pointing out over the water, the viewer's eye returned again and again to the frightening, stenciled sign posted on the beach.

Letter 1 (left)

United States Senate
COMMITTEE ON COMMERCE

November 8, 1961

Mr. Alfred R. Rochester
Executive Director
World's Fair Commission
SEATTLE WORLD'S FAIR
Seattle 9, Washington

Dear Al:

The enclosed letters from the offices of the Secretaries of State and Treasury are for your information.

Kind regards.

Sincerely,

WARREN G. MAGNUSON, U.S.S.
by direction

WGM:m

Letter 2 (right)

United States Senate
COMMITTEE ON ARMED SERVICES

October 13, 1961

Mr. Alfred R. Rochester
Executive Director
World's Fair Commission
Seattle World's Fair
Seattle 9, Washington

Dear Al:

I have the copy of your letter of October 10 to Senator Magnuson enclosing a copy of the Governor's letter of invitation to Secretary of State Rusk of October 9.

I have today written to the Secretary in an effort to encourage him to accept the Governor's cordial invitation. I am enclosing a copy of my letter for your information.

When I receive a reply from the Secretary I will be in touch with you further in this connection.

Sincerely yours,

Henry M. Jackson, U.S.S.

HMJ:a

CENTURY 21: SCOOP AND MAGGIE

Scoop and Maggie were Washington State's dynamic duo, exercising their power in Washington, DC, for four decades to bring home contracts for state businesses; money for public works projects in the state; and federal investment in various state initiatives, like the Century 21 World's Fair in Seattle. After serving in the House, Warren G. "Maggie" Magnuson was first elected to the U.S. Senate in 1944 and retained his seat until 1981. Henry M. "Scoop" Jackson successfully ran for the U.S. Senate in 1952 and served until his death in 1983. Both men were Democrats, and in their most influential years one dollar of every six budgeted by the federal government for public projects was spent in Washington State. Scoop Jackson was dubbed the "Senator from Boeing," acknowledging his role in bringing Cold War contracts to the aerospace manufacturer. Above are two of many letters from Jackson and Magnuson to Alfred Rochester and other organizers of the 1962 World's Fair. Scoop and Maggie's involvement in the planning and funding for the fair was crucial to its success.

THE FAMILY FALLOUT SHELTER

IMPROVISED SHELTERS

If a workbench is not available, you can improvise a somewhat larger shelter area by using furniture, doors, dressers, or other materials. Remove doors from their hinges and place them over supports in the corner of your basement having the best protection. The supports for the table can be chests of drawers or anything that can take a heavy load. Use two or three doors over each support for this shelter to provide sufficient strength to carry the heavy loads placed on them. Place bricks, concrete blocks, earth- or sand-filled drawers, books, a collapsible children's swimming pool filled with water, etc., over the doors to provide an overhead shield. Use anything with weight that can be moved. The heavier the material, the more the protection. The minimum weight of material to be added for each square foot over the doors is shown in the "Added Weight" box on the back cover. If a "Y" appears in the "Added Weight" box, then in order to obtain a PF of 40 in the shelter, you must place 70 pounds per square foot on top of the shelter as well as adding heavy material to the sides of the shelter to serve as a vertical shield.

Be careful not to overload the doors to the point where the shelter will collapse.

A committee of the National Academy of Sciences, in a recent study of national preparedness, concluded:

"Adequate shielding is the only effective means of preventing radiation casualties."

UNDERGROUND CONCRETE SHELTER

An underground reinforced concrete shelter can be built by a contractor for about $1,000 to $1,500, depending on the type of entrance. The shelter shown would provide almost absolute fallout protection.

Figure 10.—Pre–shaped metal shelter

If the figure entered in the box marked "Added W[e]ight" on the back cover happens to be a number such as 30, this [means that over] every square foot over the shelter area should be [placed] material having a sufficient height so as to weigh [...]. Using the weights of typical shielding materials as g[iven on page] 20, the required shielding material can be obta[ined as] following:

Approximately 3½ inches of earth or sand o[r]
Approximately 12 inches of wood or
Approximately 6 inches of water or
4-inch (nominal thickness) layer of bricks o[r]
Approximately 8 inches of library books

The shielding materials can be used individual[ly, pro]viding a 3½-inch layer of sand completely over th[e] shelter or in conjunction with other materials as [in the] illustration on the opposite page.

If vertical shielding is required (a "Y" has ap[peared in the] "Added Weight" box) this can be obtained by plac[ing ma]terial along the sides of the improvised shelter. [Place a] single course of bricks or concrete blocks, washing [machine] with water, chest of drawers filled with earth, de[ep] rows of books, etc.

GENERAL

Until the extent of the radiation threat in your [area is deter]mined by trained monitors using special instrumen[ts] stay in your shelter as much as possible. For essen[tial needs you] can leave your shelter for a few minutes. Befor[e leaving your] shelter for longer periods of time, listen to your ra[dio for] information and instructions. A battery operated [radio should] be available for this purpose.

For quick reference, after you have finished read[ing this booklet,] [cut] hang it up in the corner of your basement havin[g...]

blast, heat, and fire from the explosions would be very destructive, but the destruction would be in the areas near the explosions. Radioactive fallout, though, could spread in a thin layer over millions of square miles.

Radiation would come from the fallout wherever it settled—the ground, trees and bushes, or the roof of your home. Fallout *does not behave like a gas.* In areas that would be affected by dangerous amounts of fallout, the fallout particles would look like dirt or sand and you may see them after they have settled on the ground or other places. The exact amount of radiation given off by the particles can be measured only by special instruments.

HOW CAN YOUR PROTECTION BE IMPROVED?

There are three ways of improving your protection against fallout—time, distance, and getting some heavy material between you and the fallout (called "shielding").

1. *Time*—Radioactivity decreases rapidly at first. After an attack, the radiation would be most intense during the first few days. Even so, radiation protection may be needed for an extended period—days or weeks.

2. *Distance*—The amount of radiation is less the further away you are from the source of radiation.

3. *Shielding*—Any material that is put between a person and the source of radiation cuts down the amount of radiation that reaches the person. The thicker [the material, the] better the protec[tion].

In the event of an attack, you hav[e little control over] distance, but YOU CAN DO SO[METHING ABOUT] YOUR PROTECTION BY MEANS [OF SHIELDING.]

It is the principle of shielding t[hat the national] shelters. Under the guidance of th[e Federal Government a] system of fallout shelters is being [established throughout the] nation. It consists of public shelters [in large buildings] and home shelters.

Those community shelters having a protection factor of at least 40 and space for at least 50 people are now being marked with the familiar black and yellow shelter sign. Where necessary storage space is available, they are being stocked with food, water (if needed), sanitary and medical supplies, and radiation detection instruments. The survey is a continuing effort. Through it, a current inventory is maintained of shelters added by new construction.

The fallout protection found in homes with basements represents important additional shelter space.

Personal and other special considerations may make fallout protection at home more practical or desirable than community shelters for certain individuals or families. For example, in rural and suburban communities and even in many cities, families may live a considerable distance from the nearest community shelter. For these families, a home shelter will provide more accessible fallout protection. Fallout protection at home is usually more accessible to housewives and young children during the day and may be preferred by the whole family when at home.

HOW MUCH PROTECTION DOES YOUR BASE-MENT PROVIDE AGAINST RADIOACTIVE FALLOUT?

In homes, basement areas provide the best shelter against fallout because they are mostly belowground. This gives them a natural shield. This booklet tells you the amount of protection your basement offers and what you can do to increase this protection for your family's safety. Keep in mind that fallout shelter provides only limited protection against blast.

INTRODUCTION

Let us take a hard look at the facts.

In an atomic war, blast, heat, and initial radiation could kill millions close to ground zero of nuclear bursts.

Many *more* millions—everybody else—could be threatened by radioactive fallout. But most of these could be saved.

The purpose of this booklet is to show how to escape death from fallout.

Everyone, even those far from a likely target, would need shelter from fallout.

Your Federal Government has a shelter policy based on the knowledge that most of those beyond the range of blast and heat will survive if they have adequate protection from fallout.

This booklet contains building plans for five basic fallout shelters. One of the five—the Basement Concrete Block Shelter—has been designed specifically as a do-it-yourself project. Solid concrete blocks are used to build it. Most people probably would need the assistance of a contractor to build any of the other four types.

The least expensive shelter described is the Basement Concrete Block Shelter. The most expensive is the Underground Concrete Shelter.

Savings usually can be realized if a shelter is constructed at the time a house is being built.

Each of the shelters incorporates the fundamentals for fallout protection—shielding mass, ventilation, space to live. Each can serve a dual purpose—protection from tornadoes and other severe storms in addition to protection from the fallout radiation of a nuclear bomb.

There *are* means of protection.

But that protection must be provided before, not after, the sirens sound

Leo A. Hoegh
DIRECTOR
Office of Civil and Defense Mobilization

GROUND ZERO

In the coldest years of the Cold War, nuclear fear swept Washington State. East King County was ringed with short-range Nike missile sites, designed to intercept incoming bombers. In 1960, King County Civil Defense toured shopping centers and libraries with a mock family fallout shelter—a "fall-out and blast survival station," as it was termed. Excerpted here are instructions and illustrations from *The Family Fallout Shelter*, published in 1959 by the Office of Civil and Defense Mobilization, and *Fallout Protection for Homes with Basements*, published in 1967 by the Office of Civil Defense, within the Department of Defense. Both brochures, with many others produced by Washington State and by various counties, were widely distributed at demonstrations throughout the state. The Puget Sound Navy Yard, the Boeing Company sites, Hanford, and the many military bases in Washington State were logical targets for missiles, and the wind-borne radioactive fallout from those nuclear attacks would contaminate large areas. It is unknown how many Washington State families prepared for the unthinkable by building a fallout shelter in their basement, garage, or backyard, or stockpiled food and water, expecting to wait out the aftermath of a nuclear attack.

COLD WAR ON PUGET SOUND

In the early 1960s grassroots radical right organizations like the John Birch Society enjoyed considerable popularity throughout the nation, and in Washington State. In 1962 Reverend Fred Schwartz brought the Puget Sound School of Anti-Communism to King County, under the umbrella of the Christian Anti-Communist Crusade. The school's classes included the "Philosophy of Communism," "Communism and Education," and "How to Debate with Communists and Fellow Travelers." A number of local elected officials endorsed the school, and periodicals as diverse as *Catholic Northwest Progress* and the *Boeing News* provided approving advance publicity for the classes. When the Bellevue school board's agenda took up the matter of the Puget Sound School of Anti-Communism, six hundred parents attended the school board meeting where Reverend Schwartz gave an impromptu lecture to the crowd. According to the *Bellevue American* (February 8, 1962), the board reluctantly accepted the opinion of its attorney that the district could not offer teachers release time to attend the school. The board president quit that spring, disgusted with what he called "pseudo psychological influences" on educators in the district. Suspect teaching methods included sight-reading, math manipulatives, open classrooms, and ungraded instruction. Parents were encouraged to be suspicious of their children's teachers, and a Mercer Island John Birch Society organizer told a *Seattle Times* reporter on March 29, 1961, "I don't see anything wrong in asking children to report if their teachers are teaching communism."

CENTURY 21'S WORLD OF TOMORROW

Century 21 planners boldly envisioned a world's fair in Seattle in 1962 that would imagine and invent the twenty-first century on a global scale. Ten million visitors came to the little city on Puget Sound that aspired to be the international capital of innovation. From the start, the fairgrounds were intended to be Seattle's postfair center for the arts, sports, and entertainment. Much of the exposition remains today, from the Monorail and the Space Needle to the International Fountain, the Coliseum, and the Pacific Science Center, providing an enduring sense of place for memories of the fair. Lavishly supported by the National Science Foundation and federal appropriations, Century 21 included exhibits and pavilions, sculptures and fountains, the futuristic Space Needle and the model technology of the monorail. Organizers worked to internationalize this Cold War exposition, unsuccessfully urging the Union of Soviet Socialist Republics and other Iron Curtain countries to participate. Throughout its run, Century 21 was characterized by contesting themes of internationalism and provincialism, sophistication and parochialism, sunny optimism and the deepest dread—all framing visions of the twenty-first century rooted firmly in 1962.

SEATTLE'S CENTURY 21 IS SLIPPING PAST
...ENDING BEFORE IT BEGINS ELSEWHERE

GEORGE KUTI
1962

SEATTLE WORLD'S FAIR POSES CHALLENGE TO MAN

SEATTLE WORLD'S FAIR 1962

PHOTO

RECORD

PLAY RECORD AT 33⅓ RPM MANUAL

CHARTER MEMBER
CENTURY 21 EXPOSITION
MONORAIL MILER
World's first high speed, mass transit Monorail

AMERICA'S SPACE AGE WORLD'S FAIR
Seattle, U.S.A.—April 21-October 21, 1962

GRACIE HANSEN'S
Paradise!
INTERNATIONAL MUSICAL REVUE
234 10TH AVENUE EAST • SEATTLE 2, WASH.

America's Space Age World's Fair
Seattle, U.S.A.   April 21-October 21, 1962

HIGH FIDELITY
SEE YOU IN SEATTLE
(at the Big World's Fair)
BY THE LANCERS

Words and Music by
TUBBY CLARK
BEN HARKINS
VIRGINIA BURNSIDE

THEME SONG
SEATTLE
WORLD'S FAIR

The Rose

I

There are those to whom place is unimportant,
But this place, where sea and fresh water meet,
Is important:
Where the hawks sway out into the wind,
Without a single wing-beat,
And the gulls cry against the crows
In the curved harbors,
And the tide rises up against the grass
Nibbled by sheep and rabbits.

A time for watching the tide,
For the heron's hieratic fishing,
For the sleepy cries of the towhee,
The morning birds gone, the twittering finches,
But still the flash of the kingfisher, the wing-beat of the scoter,
The sun a ball of fire coming down over the water,
The last geese crossing against the reflected after-light,
The moon retreating into a vague cloud-shape
To the cries of the owl, the eerie whooper.
The old log subsides with the lessening waves,
And there is silence.

I sway outside myself
Into the darkening currents,
Into the small spillage of driftwood,
The waters swirling past the tiny headlands.

ROETHKE'S "THE ROSE"

Theodore Roethke joined the faculty of the University of Washington in 1947; he taught there until his death in the summer of 1963. Roethke was awarded the Pulitzer Prize for poetry in 1954 and a National Book Award in 1959, both while he was teaching at the university. Here you see two versions of one stanza of his poem "The Rose"—first, a very rough early draft, and second, the polished, typed transcript, showing the creative arc of this work of art. Roethke's widow mentioned to me in email that the inspiration for the poem came from a wild rose the poet observed on San Juan Island. Roethke read the entire poem aloud in a performance at the Playhouse at Century 21, on October 14, 1962. In a prereading interview, Roethke told *Seattle Times* interviewer Bill Schear that he had stayed in Seattle because "the University of Washington's English Department is the best in the country . . . [and] I get some of the best students in the world." On the following day, *Times* writer Louis Guzzo published a glowing review of the reading, pointing out that "Roethke's love affair with the Northwest grows in passion and compassion," particularly citing "The Rose," which Guzzo called "a lyrical, soaring tribute to the land, sea and skies of what has been his home . . . since 1947."

AN OLD COWBOY

Below you see both sides of a postcard. When the card was originally published, in 1967, this cowboy and his skills seemed to be fast slipping away. Artist Larry George captured perfectly the ease and confidence of this Old Cowboy, a Native friend of his. George was an artist, storyteller, muralist, and lecturer who lived in Toppenish, on the Yakama Indian Reservation. Larry George received the Governor's Heritage Award, honoring his contributions to the preservation of traditional Native-American culture in Washington State.

Post Card

By Acme Printers, 636 Decatur Avenue, Sunnyside, Washington

COWBOY. The subject is an old cowboy friend of the artist, Larry A. George of Toppenish, Washington. Mr. George is a young artist of great potential and shows promise of being one of America's outstanding native Indian artists.

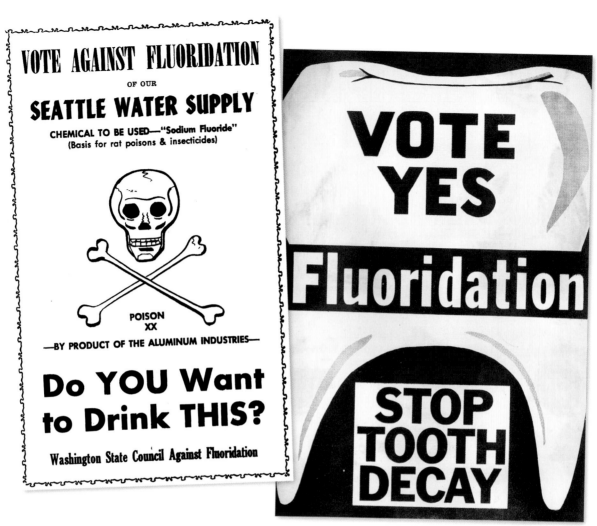

IT'S IN THE WATER

Municipal fluoridation of the public drinking water supply has so dramatically decreased the incidence of tooth decay that it is difficult to imagine a time when fluoridation was the subject of heated controversy. Today the U.S. Centers for Disease Control and Prevention consider fluoridation one of the ten most significant twentieth-century public health achievements. However, in the 1950s and '60s, some opponents of fluoridation opposed the wholesale administration of this chemical, which they considered a poison. Others objected to the violation of individual rights for what was held to be the public good—socialism. The controversy, embodied in the two posters shown above, made *Time* magazine, March 10, 1952, in an article that poked fun at Seattle. University of Washington engineering professor Ernest Engle was quoted: "Who endorses fluoridation? Why, the different state agencies, the U.S. Public Health Service and others who are working for socialized medicine in a welfare state." The *Time* article went on to describe the visit of a group of antifluoridationists to the University of Washington. They wanted to inspect all available skulls of Puget Sound Indians, to study their teeth and see how the original residents of Seattle had gotten along without fluoridated water. Then, as *Time* put it, "A university instructor pointed out that the Puget Sound Indians lived almost entirely on seafood, rich in that sinister chemical, fluorine." This controversy lingered for more than a decade, and Seattle voters did not approve fluoridation of their drinking water until 1968.

SPOKANE COUNTERCULTURE

The *Spokane Natural* was an underground newspaper, published from May 5, 1967 through November 13, 1970. Initially coedited by Russ Nobbs and Ormond Otvos, this issue noted that the paper was published by the Mandala Print Shoppe and was a member of the Underground Press Syndicate (UPS)—both items indicated on the cover. On April 7, 1967, the *Spokane Daily Chronicle* published an article about the *Natural*. The *Chronicle* reporter interviewed Nobbs and Otvos about their "hippie mission," a converted barbershop storefront and bookstore at 522 South Cannon Street. The young men said they moved to Spokane from California because they considered the city "super right-wing" and they "hoped to fill an information gap" in Spokane, which was badly in need of a "new community." Additionally, Nobbs and Otvos hoped to promote the local counterculture arts scene, from folk rock and soul music to the work of visual artists of every sort. Russ Nobbs soon became sole editor of the *Spokane Natural*, and the newspaper's circulation grew to three thousand copies. Nobbs donated his entire set of newspaper copies, photographic negatives, paste-ups and the original hand-cranked Gestetner mimeograph machine to the Northwest Museum of Arts and Culture, Spokane.

WASHINGTON'S WOODSTOCK

On March 23, 1967, Seattle's *Helix* published its first issue. Founded and edited by Paul Dorpat, *Helix* was Seattle's first underground newspaper and the principal counterculture voice of the Pacific Northwest. Beautifully designed, *Helix* covered radical culture, promoted antiwar activism, and helped to organize be-ins, rallies, and music festivals. It had a circulation of eighteen thousand at its peak. Published through June 11, 1970, *Helix* included the early work of Walt Crowley as cartoonist, writer and editor; Tom Robbins; and many others. Here you see the full-page advertisement for the first Sky River Rock Festival, which took place near the Skykomish River in Sultan, August 31 to September 2, 1968. Walt Crowley drew this poster, complete with a marijuana joint–smoking toad, that bills the event as a benefit "for American Indians and black Americans." The list of expected entertainers featured nationally known performers and bands as well as local ones, but the mainstream press was much more interested in who attended the festival than who played at it. With fascinated horror, the *Everett Herald* reported on Sky River on September 2: "With Betty 'Universal Mother' Nelson's organic raspberry farm the Mecca, thousands of them came this weekend, [and] who are they? Hippies - all sizes, shapes, skins and scents." Out in Sultan, about twenty thousand attendees camped, played, and danced to great music over Labor Day weekend 1968. *Helix* helped to create the Sky River Rock Festival and set the stage for Woodstock in the summer of 1969.

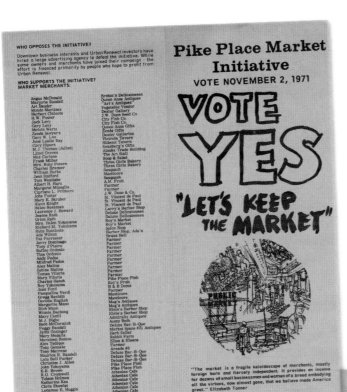

Pike Place Market Initiative
VOTE NOVEMBER 2, 1971

VOTE YES
"LET'S KEEP THE MARKET"

"The market is a fragile kaleidoscope of merchants, mostly foreign born and fiercely independent. It provides an income for dozens of small businessmen and women of a breed embodying all the virtues, now almost gone, that we believe made America great." Elizabeth Tonner

FRIENDS of the MARKET
Victor Steinbrueck, Pres.

...TRUTH ABOUT THE MARKET INITIATIVE

...market buildings show signs of recent neglect, the ...ctures are sound and regularly pass all health, building ...department inspections. The market is healthy and ...d business has been constantly improving. The Market ...oration and rehabilitation - not demolition.

...rom 45 farms is sold in the Market now despite the disinterest of the City and the owners. City regulations limit participation to residents of King, Kitsap and Pierce Counties. Many new farmer tenants could be attracted from the largely rural Snohomish and Skagit Counties if the regulation were dropped.

- The Market Initiative will not kill Urban Renewal. It forces use of Urban Renewal funds to preserve and restore the Market. The initiative affects only 7 of the 22 acres in the project. The initiative will force modification of the plan - but Federal Officials state that funds for renovation will be available if the City wishes to proceed when the Initiative passes.

- The Initiative will encourage renovation. The Market Initiative is patterned after the Pioneer Square Historic Ordinance. Passage of that ordinance has stabilized the area and owners have engaged in improvement and renovation with renewed confidence. Federal Historic preservation funds would be available in the Market when the Market Initiative passes.

- The Market Initiative is supported by 85 merchants and businessmen in the Market. The Initiative is opposed by those owners who wish to sell out to Urban Renewal. It is supported by merchants who wish to see the Market continue.

WHAT IS THE INITIATIVE?

The Initiative creates a Market Historic District.

The purpose is to preserve, improve and restore the Pike Place Market area.

A representative Historic District Commission would control demolition and construction and encourage marketing activities.

Changes and improvements appropriate to the character and purpose of the Market would be encouraged.

The present Pike Plaza Urban Renewal plan will be required to be modified to truly preserve and continue the Market.

WHY AN INITIATIVE?

Buildings in the area have been neglected due to the uncertainty created by urban renewal.

The Market Initiative will stabilize the area and require appropriate modification of present urban renewal plans.

The people's Pike Place Market as we know it would not survive without realistic controls.

Urban Renewal would replace familiar market businesses such as the Sanitary Market, garden and thrift stores, and many of the farmers' stalls with high-rise apartments and a hotel, and a 4000 car garage.

Contemplated renovation would triple rents for the remaining merchants.

SAVE THE MARKET!

Since its opening in 1907 the Pike Place Market has become synonymous with Seattle. Its stalls offer the products of small farmers, bakers, and craftspeople in a rich and interesting place where shoppers and tourists get to "Meet the Producer." In the 1960s some judged the Market to be seedy and run-down, and in need of "urban renewal." A proposal was developed to essentially demolish the Market and replace it with Pike Plaza, including an upscale hotel, apartment building, four office towers, and a huge parking garage. This proposal gained wide support from Seattle's political and business leadership—indeed, from many who were eager for modernity and saw no value in historic preservation. The Friends of the Market fought back, placing an initiative on the ballot to create a historic district for preservation and public management of the Pike Place Market. This brochure, produced by Friends of the Market, encouraged a yes vote on the November 2 ballot initiative in 1971. Victor Steinbrueck—architect, educator, public intellectual, and activist—served as president of Friends of the Market and drew the circular collage to express the Market's rich identity. Earlier, introducing his brilliant *Market Sketchbook* (University of Washington Press, 1968), Steinbrueck wrote, "Seattle's Pike Place Market deserves more than a book; it deserves to live on, as a link with Seattle's past, a meaningful and much-loved part of its present and a place of unlimited possibilities for its future." Today the Seattle Department of Neighborhoods recognizes a seven-acre Pike Place Market Historical District.

GET THE U.S. OUT OF VIETNAM!

In the late 1960s and into the 1970s, Washington State activists staged widespread protest demonstrations. Protestors resisted what they saw as the Establishment's effort to maintain "business as usual" when the Vietnam War was escalating and there was no fair access to housing, education, and jobs for people of color back home. Activists worked hard for Earth Day, for the liberation of women, for access to medical care for all, and for the rights of Native American people in Washington State. Their activities ranged across a wide spectrum, from peaceful protest to civil disobedience to violence and destruction of property. These documents were gathered in files labeled "Incident Reports" in the collection of the federal Public Buildings Service. However, the files also include ephemera—for instance, these two flyers, one for a mass peaceful May demonstration in downtown Seattle, and the second for a meeting at the University of Washington Husky Union Building to prepare for a demonstration on November 6, 1970. That was the expected opening date for the trial of the Seattle Seven—members of the Seattle Liberation Front, a radical anti-Vietnam War organization—who had been indicted by a federal grand jury and charged with inciting a riot in February 1970 at Seattle's federal courthouse. Threats to federal property prompted infiltration of antiwar groups by spies who yielded the "intelligence" referred to in these reports, which threaten or document violence against government buildings in cities across the state, from Seattle to Bellingham, Tacoma to Spokane.

stop the bombing! end the blockade!

out now!

When Nixon announced his decision to blockade North Vietnam and escalate the bombing, he made a special plea to the American people to support him. He said, "It is you, most of all, that the world will be watching." The world is watching--to see if we will allow Nixon to get away with his bloody escalation of the war which contains within it the threat of world war and nuclear destruction. On the night of Nixon's speech, and the following day, thousands took to the streets to express opposition at Nixon's action. These protests must only be the beginning. We must continue this revolt against the war, drawing ever larger numbers of people into protest against it. The antiwar movement has forced Nixon to withdraw 200,000 ground troops from Vietnam. We have the power to stop this new escalation if we act to end it. Join with us May 21 in a continuing protest against the war.

mass peaceful demonstration

sun. may 21 1:pm federal courthouse

5th & Madison

SEATTLE PEACE ACTION COALITION
STUDENT MOBILIZATION COMMITTEE
WASHINGTON DEMOCRATIC COUNCIL
CAM

For more

ON TO NOV. 6

Volunteers Needed!

Seattle Peace Action Coalition 1406 ne 50th• LA 2-2222

Come to the next SEAPAC meeting.

Sunday OCT. 17 8:00 pm U of W HUB

GUEST SPEAKER-- STEPHANIE COONTZ
A member of the National Coordinating Committee of the National Peace Action Coalition. Coontz is on a national speaking tour to build the November 6 regional demonstrations and report on the October 13 Moratorium.

INCIDENT REPORT

-//c

FOR COMPLETION OF THIS FORM, SEE REVERSE SIDE

1. INFORMATION RECEIVED FROM:

A. NAME David Reed

B. TITLE Assistant Field Office Manager

C. LOCATION Spokane, WA

D. DATE & TIME 4-21-72 8:45 a.m.

2. TYPE OF INCIDENT

Pending Demonstration

3. FACILITY WHERE INCIDENT OCCURRED:

A. NAME U.S. Court House 46-0064

B. ADDRESS Spokane, WA

C. GOV'T OWNED [X]   LEASED [ ]

D. NET SQ. FT. 192,290

E. NUMBER OF OCCUPANTS 504

F. MAJOR OCCUPANT AGENCY Soil Conservation Service

G. JURISDICTION   EX [x] CON [ ] PROP [ ] PART [ ]

4. DETAILS OF INCIDENT

Mr. Reed reported that students from Gonzaga University who call themselves the "Spokane People for Peace" plan a demonstration for 12 noon, Saturday, April 22, 1972. The target of the demonstration is the U.S. Air Force because of the renewed bombing of North VietNam, with an unknown number of persons expected to participate. Unqualified information received indicates the possibility of some trouble. Local police have been notified and will be available. Necessary overtime for FPOs has been approved from this headquarters, and Mr. Innamorati, Assistant Commissioner for Buildings Management, Central Office.

TO:

Eml 10PBP

SUBJECT: Planned Demonstrations

BUILDING

LOCATION Seattle, WA

NET SQ. FT. | NO. OF OCCUPANTS | [ ] GOV'T OWNED | [ ] LEASED | JURISDICTION

MESSAGE:

11-3-71 9 a.m. Capt. R. J. Major reported the following: The People's Coalition for Peace and Justice are passing out fill-in type questionaires at the U. of W. today, asking for individual preference for Nov. 6 - do they want a march, rally, or cultural event? They are also advising that there will be workshops on Sunday, Nov. 7, subjects: prisons, welfare, feminism, politics, 1972 elections, imperialism, and Indo-China. They are advertising "No business as usual on Nov. 8." They are asking for the people's preference for the 8th. The choices are civil disobedience, picketing Safeway Stores, street speakers, or guerilla theater. They are also making a plea for donations. The general projection is that they are pushing real hard for success on Saturday Nov. 6. If they have good attendance they very possibly will continue through Sunday and Monday.

ON OCTOBER TWENTYSEVEN, SEVENTYONE, A SOURCE WHO HAS FURNISHED RELIABLE INFORMATION IN THE PAST, REPORTED THE SEATTLE PEACE ACTION COALITION, AN AFFILIATE OF THE TROTSKYIST NATIONAL PEACE ACTION COALITION, IS CALLING FOR A LARGE-SCALE DEMONSTRATION, WHICH WILL ASSEMBLE AT THE FEDERAL COURT HOUSE IN SEATTLE, WASHINGTON, AT TWELVE NOON, NOVEMBER SIX NEXT. THE GROUP WILL THEN MARCH TO VOLUNTEER PARK FOR A RALLY AT TWO PM.

PLANS ARE BEING WORKED ON TO HAVE TWENTY BUSLOADS OF PERSONS FROM PORTLAND, OREGON, JOIN THE SEATLE DEMONSTRATORS. NO SPECIFICS ON THE PORTLAND DELEGATION NOW KNOWN.

ABOVE FURNISHED TO U. S. ATTORNEY, SECRET SERVICE, U. S. MARSHAL, GENERAL SERVICES ADMINISTRATION, ARMY INTELLIGENCE AND SEATTLE POLICE.

November 5, 1971

10PF-16

Possible demonstration

The Record

Mr. Clancy called at 8:50 a.m. with information that a faction of the weathermen will be causing a disturbance this weekend, according to information received by the Federal Protective Service. The particular group is known as the "Flame of the West," and information indicated that they will center their attention on the oil industry and attempt destruction of Federal Buildings and installations. The information will be relayed to the Federal Regional Center, Bothell, and to the Public Buildings Service Building in Tacoma. Additionally, the Fire Department at the Auburn facility will be alerted.

B. C. HANSON
Auburn Field Office Manager
Buildings Management Division

INCIDENT REPORT

Eml

FOR COMPLETION OF THIS FORM, SEE REVERSE SIDE

1. INFORMATION RECEIVED FROM:

A. NAME Curtis Ray

B. TITLE Field Office Manager

C. LOCATION Bellingham, WA

D. DATE & TIME 3/31/72 8:15 am

2. TYPE OF INCIDENT

Scheduled demonstration

3. FACILITY WHERE INCIDENT OCCURRED:

A. NAME Peace Arch Border Station 46-0006

B. ADDRESS Blaine, WA

C. GOV'T OWNED [X]   LEASED [ ]

D. NET SQ. FT. 13,855

E. NUMBER OF OCCUPANTS 60

F. MAJOR OCCUPANT AGENCY Treasury/Customs

G. JURISDICTION   EX [x] CON [ ] PROP [ ] PART [ ]

4. DETAILS OF INCIDENT

At 2 p.m. 3/31/72, a demonstration will be held, sponsored by Viet Nam Veterans, British Columbia Peace Council, The League for Corrective Action, The Viet Nam Action Committee and the U.S. Trotskyites at the Peace Arch between the U.S. and Canada. Six thousand people are expected to participate in this peaceful demonstration. The Whatcom County Sheriff, U.S. Border Patrol, Washington State Patrol, Immigration & Naturalization Service, and U.S. Customs have been advised.

ROUTING SLIP

TO	CO	R1	R2	R3	R4	R5	R6	R7	R8	R9	R10
NAME/TITLE						CORRESPONDENCE SYMBOL					
1.											
2. 10PB											
3.						HOLD					
4.											
5.											

[ ] ALLOTMENT SYMBOL [ ] HANDLE DIRECT [ ] READ AND DESTROY
[ ] APPROVAL [ ] IMMEDIATE ACTION [ ] RECOMMENDATION
[ ] AS REQUESTED [ ] INITIALS [ ] SEE ME
[ ] CONCURRENCE [ ] NECESSARY ACTION [ ] SIGNATURE
[ ] CORRECTION [ ] NOTE AND RETURN [ ] YOUR COMMENT
[ ] FILING [ ] PER OUR CONVERSATION [ ] YOUR INFORMATION
[ ] FULL REPORT [ ] PER TELEPHONE CONVERSATION
[ ] ANSWER OR ACKNOWLEDGE ON OR BEFORE ___
[ ] PREPARE REPLY FOR THE SIGNATURE OF

REMARKS

Several times recently, we have received information too late to be of benefit to us. Following Mr. Cadigan's suggestion to reduce or eliminate unnecessary information from going to the Regional Administrator, the need-to-know criteria should be instituted.

The FBI and other police agencies prefer to notify the action agency initially. Therefore, it is suggested that this type information be routed directly to the FPSB for action and dissemination to all concerned of the problem and action taken.

FROM | CO | R1 | R2 | R3 | R4 | R5 | R6 | R7 | R8 | R9 | R10
NAME/TITLE Eml 10PBP | CORR. SYMBOL | BUILDING, ROOM, ETC.
| TELEPHONE | DATE

U. S. GOVERNMENT PRINTING OFFICE: 1969 O - 355-522 (4134) 887-980   GSA FORM 14   JUN 67

---

ureau of Investigation
, Washington
ber 2, 1971

or

inistrations
er

8002

PEACE ACTION COALITION
ION CONCERNING

mation, I am enclosing communications
to you.

Very truly yours,

J. E. MILNES
Special Agent in Charge

closures, if any, this transmittal form becomes

Ransom money in the amount $200,000 was made up entirely of used, random 20 dollar bills. It was obtained from the Seattle-First National Bank, Main Office, and was part of a ransom package of $250,000, which had been maintained by the bank for such emergencies.

The money was delivered from the bank to the Seattle-Tacoma International Airport (Sea-Tac), by two bank employees; Mr. WILLIAM C. GRINNELL and Mr. FRANK J. BURNS, both employed as Investigators, Security Department, Seattle-First National Bank, who were transported from the bank to the airport in an unmarked Seattle Police Department vehicle, driven by Detective OWEN C. MC KENNA.

The money was delivered to Northwest Airlines (NWA), at Sea-Tac, where the bank officials handed it to Mr. AL LEE, Director of Flying, Western Region, NWA.

The money was later delivered to the plane by the same unmarked Seattle Police Department vehicle by Mr. LEE and Detective MC KENNA. The money was then handed over to Stewardess TINA MUCKLOW, who delivered it to the hijacker on board the aircraft.

The entire list of the ransom bills had previously been microfilmed by the Seattle-First National Bank, and has now been incorporated in a 34 page pamphlet of ransom bills.

Based upon information received from the Seattle Division on November 25, 1971 preliminary steps were taken to alert all law enforcement agencies in Cowlitz, Lewis, Wahkiakum, and Clark Counties concerning the search which was to be instituted for the subject. A meeting was held with members of the Clark and Cowlitz County Sheriff's Offices and local agencies at the Woodland, Washington City Hall and Police Department which was designated as search headquarters in view of its proximity to the Woodland airport at which facilities were available for fixed wing aircraft and helicopters. Arrangements were made for helicopters and fixed wing aircraft to be available on November 26, 1971 and the search area was divided into seven sections, one of which was located in the Lewis River area of Cowlitz County and the others in the northeastern section of Clark County.

0713 GMT   11:13 PM, PST

RNO TWR LC: NORTHWEST THREE ZERO FIVE RENO TOWER DO NOT TOUCH ANYTHING ABOARD THE AIRCRAFT EXIT THE AIRCRAFT FROM THE FRONT DO NOT TOUCH ANYTHING ABOARD THE AIRCRAFT AND EXIT FROM THE FRONT

NW305:   AH RENO RENO THIS IS NORTHWEST AH THREE ZERO FIVE

RNO TWR LC: NORTHWEST THREE ZERO FIVE RENO TOWER

NW305:   OKAY SIR BE ADVISED THAT AH WE APPARENTLY AH OUR PASSENGER TOOK LEAVE OF US SOMEWHERE AH BETWEEN HERE AND SEATTLE WE HAVE AH MADE A RATHER CURSORY EXAMINATION OF THE AIRCRAFT FOR THE AH BRIEF CASE

– 223 –

Probable Bail Out Point of Hijacker

WITHOUT A TRACE

Here are excerpts from the Federal Bureau of Investigation file on the man known to us as D. B. Cooper. On November 24, 1971, a passenger who had identified himself to the ticket agent as Dan Cooper hijacked a Boeing 727 while en route from Portland to Seattle. Cooper handed a flight attendant a note that read in part, "I have a bomb in my briefcase. I will use it if necessary. I want you to sit next to me. You are being hijacked," and demanded $200,000. He insisted that the plane not land at Seattle-Tacoma International Airport until the money and parachutes were ready and waiting. There, the passengers and some crew members were released, and an airline employee made the delivery to the plane. After refueling the 727, Cooper ordered the pilot to fly to Mexico, and told all onboard crewmembers to stay in the cockpit, leaving him alone in the unpressurized cabin. At some point, Dan Cooper opened the aft door and jumped from the plane with a parachute and the money. Cooper's true identity and what became of him remain unknown, and most of the ransom money has never been found in the only unsolved aircraft hijacking in U.S. history. Against the grim backdrop of the Boeing Bust, Cooper seemed a folk hero to some—a man who risked his life to gain a small fortune.

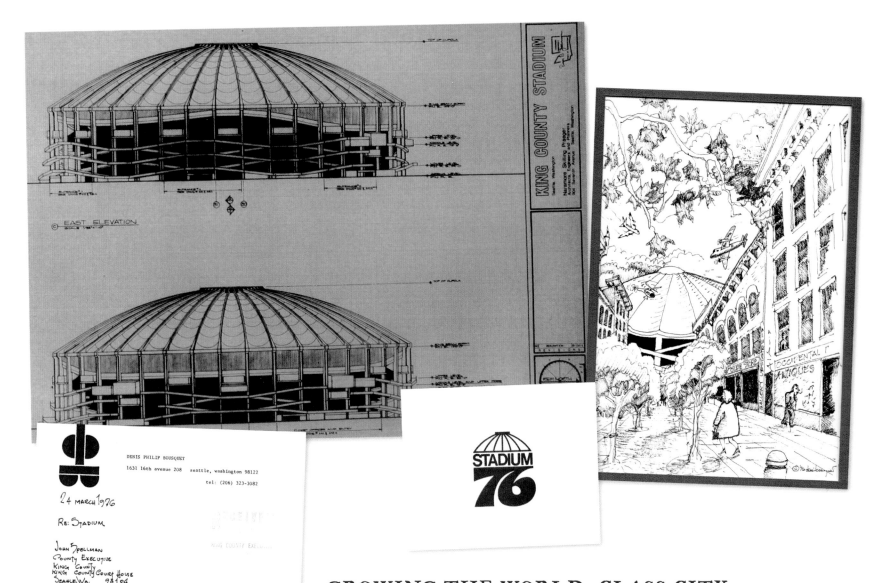

GROWING THE WORLD-CLASS CITY

In 1968 a citizens group, Forward Thrust, placed a set of ballot measures before King County voters, who rejected mass transit but approved acquisition of park land and the construction of a multipurpose domed stadium, soon to be known as the Kingdome. Construction began in 1972 on the largest freestanding concrete dome in the world. Initially known as Stadium 76, the Kingdome was soon home to the Seattle Seahawks, Mariners, and SuperSonics. Although the stadium was created to further Seattle's aspirations to be a "world-class city," the location of the Kingdome in the International District drew criticism. The letter and drawing shown satirize this mammoth, brooding "wonder of engineering without architecture" that dwarfed its neighborhood. The stadium was demolished in 2000 and replaced by two arenas. The elevation shows the east and north exteriors of the Kingdome as they were originally constructed.

especially after the previous summer's events. But it was difficult. It's difficult to be tough enough to take a stand and get things done, and still be moderate. It takes people like me who prepare the way and take the beating—that's what you've got to have.

Even though I hadn't wanted to be there, I was ripe for the city council. I felt free of party pressure. I saw myself in a different setting, and I saw a different need. I saw that something had to be done to ignite the fire in the city to do something. The city hadn't done anything, hadn't stepped up to meet the challenge, because nobody on the city council knew what to do. And I was fresh and brimming over with ideas. And the people just fell in behind me.

I had an open wing of liberals who were supporting me, and it was like they were happy to see me on the scene. But I had to do something to attract my black supporters who had been unhappy because I left the Legislature. They felt that they lost ground, which they did. The Legislature was fully white after I left because the Democratic Party appointed Dan O'Donnell to fill my seat. But we remedied that by putting George Fleming in there after the first election.

I wasn't the spokesman for the black community. I was trying to quiet the black community, so that we could have a peaceful situation and make progress. But my constituency was no longer limited to the Thirty-seventh District. My constituency was citywide. And my goal was always to represent all of the people, and to work for the improvement of the total city. But I couldn't ignore the black community's problems. I kept track of protest by moving in among the people—general, ordinary people who were my former Thirty-seventh District constituents. I mixed in with the protesters, black and white, anti-war and civil rights. I had conversations with them, and I picked up their strong feelings.

Nobody wanted a riot in the city of Seattle. But we were getting awfully close. Nobody was prepared for what was happening across the country, because we had never experienced it. So everybody was flying blind. Because nobody was

prepared, nobody had any idea of what we were going to be faced with. There was a real fear of the unknown. Fear of the unknown, that was the fact. The pure fact of the unknown. And, as I told you, that was part of the movement to get me to the city council, a position that I didn't want at first. But I saw the sense of it later on. The idea was we didn't have anybody in the city council who had any experience, who had any connection with the community, so we'd better get someone there and get them there first before the explosiveness reached the city.

Seattle had been a city—up until the protests started in the South—that was free of obvious participation in racism. The black neighborhoods certainly were not on the verge of exploding. Later, it spread like wildfire; it just caught on after the explosions in other cities. But the leaders of Seattle were trying to make progress. They wanted the racism to be out of the city. They didn't encourage it all. So it was a model city, measured by other cities.

And the city succeeded by electing me. And you know, pardon me for being boastful, but with my moving to the city council, the reporting activity centered on a city councilman the first year—not so much the Legislature. This affected people's awareness.

Here in Seattle, my election was a victory for change on the council. A newspaper article stated that voters were angry at the approach of the council before we were there. Phyllis Lamphere, Tim, and myself were voted in to break tradition. I agree with that. We broke up the city council being made up of members all over fifty-five. We stopped that trend. I was forty-five and Tim was in his thirties, and Phyllis was about my age. We were reasonably young. And I felt early on that we would change Seattle. I felt that was the start of the reform movement that would gather steam. And it did.

The voters had lost all confidence in the old city council to take care of any problems. When I first got to the city council, I remember Phyllis, Tim and I were described by the press as the reform group. At first I didn't know what they

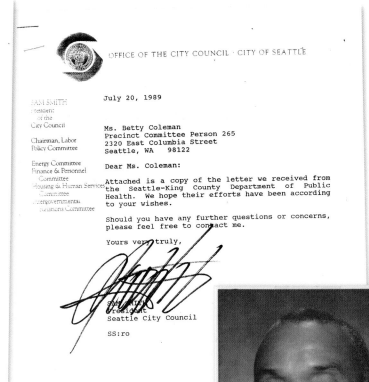

July 20, 1989

Ms. Betty Coleman
Precinct Committee Person 265
2320 East Columbia Street
Seattle, WA 98122

Dear Ms. Coleman:

Attached is a copy of the letter we received from the Seattle-King County Department of Public Health. We hope their efforts have been according to your wishes.

Should you have any further questions or concerns, please feel free to contact me.

Yours very truly,

SAM SMITH
President
Seattle City Council

SS:ro

600 Fourth Avenue, Municipal B
Seattle, Washington 98104 (206) 6

EVERYONE'S NEIGHBOR

In 1958 Sam Smith was elected to the state House of Representatives from Seattle's Thirty-Seventh District, serving five consecutive terms. Smith achieved his goal of passing a state open housing law in 1967, and he then left the state legislature to run for the Seattle City Council. Smith was the first black person to be elected to the council and served there for twenty-four years, including eight years as council president. Smith joined the Seattle City Council during an era of dramatic change, as new faces appeared at the table to develop and pursue an innovative civic agenda with fresh transparency and accountability. Sam Smith was a consummate politician and a man of integrity and principle. Above you see a brief excerpt from his extensive oral history, published in 2000, as well as his portrait and his forceful signature.

All over the world Boeing jetliners are getting people together.

BOEING 737

Boeing passenger jets have made our world smaller—bringing China, Tehran, and Paris closer to one another, and closer to New York and Seattle—by designing and building generations of planes that provide air travel faster, more conveniently, and less expensively. This advertisement for the Boeing 737 appeared in magazines and newspapers throughout the United States in 1973. The 737 is the best-selling passenger jet in the history of aviation; it has been in continuous production since 1967, with nearly ten thousand sold or on order. The statistics are absolutely staggering: at any given moment, an average of more than twelve hundred 737s are airborne, and one departs or lands somewhere on the planet every five seconds.

EXPO '74

In 1974 Spokane hosted a world's fair, the smallest city ever to do so. Over its six-month run, more than five million people visited the hundred-acre fairgrounds. The theme for Expo '74 was "Celebrating Tomorrow's Fresh New Environment," and Expo '74's opening day was marked by the release of 1974 trout into the Spokane River in order to prove that the once-polluted river had been cleaned up enough to support fish life. Planners also took advantage of the opportunity offered by the fair to completely demolish and then redevelop the old industrial heart of the city, on the islands and banks of the Spokane River. At the close of the fair, Spokane's Riverfront Park was the event's lasting legacy, where the clock tower of the Great Northern Railway station remained standing as well as the Washington State Pavilion and the U.S. Pavilion. Expo '74 offered Spokane the opportunity to reinvent itself, and to host a thoughtful fair that developed new understandings about environmental responsibility.

OFFICIAL SOUVENIR PROGRAM

expo'74 World's Fair
Spokane, USA May 4 - Nov 3, 1974

$2.00
$1.90 PLUS 10¢ TAX

SOVIET PAVILION

SPOKANE, USA, MAY—NOVEMBER '74

USSR EXPO'74

THE BOLDT DECISION

The treaties that were concluded with Native tribes throughout Washington Territory listed some obligations that were casually agreed to in 1854 and 1855, assuming that Native people would either assimilate or disappear. In 1974 those assumptions were proven wrong. One treaty right reserved to Native people was that of "taking fish at all usual and accustomed grounds . . . in common with all citizens of the territory." Disagreement between white sport and commercial fishermen and Indian fishermen over the meaning of these phrases grew increasingly strident. Bill Frank Sr.'s determination to fish as his ancestors had done, at Frank's Landing on the Nisqually River south of Tacoma, became the focus for organized protests. Adopting the contemporary tools of civil disobedience, Frank and others staged "fish-ins" that involved Hollywood actors and Las Vegas comedians. The 1974 decision of U.S. District Judge George Boldt confirmed that Indian fishermen were entitled to fifty percent of the annual catch of salmon in Washington State.

COPY

FILED IN THE
UNITED STATES DISTRICT COURT
WESTERN DISTRICT OF WASHINGTON

UNITED STATES DISTRICT COURT
WESTERN DISTRICT OF WASHINGTON
AT TACOMA

FEB 12 1974

EDGAR SCOFIELD, CLERK

By _____ Deputy

UNITED STATES OF AMERICA,

    Plaintiff,

QUINAULT TRIBE OF INDIANS on its own behalf and on behalf of the QUEETS BAND OF INDIANS; MAKAH INDIAN TRIBE; LUMMI INDIAN TRIBE; HOH TRIBE OF INDIANS; MUCKLESHOOT INDIAN TRIBE; SQUAXIN ISLAND TRIBE OF INDIANS; SAUK-SUIATTLE INDIAN TRIBE; SKOKOMISH INDIAN TRIBE; CONFEDERATED TRIBES AND BANDS OF THE YAKIMA INDIAN NATION; UPPER SKAGIT RIVER TRIBE; STILLAGUAMISH TRIBE OF INDIANS; and QUILEUTE INDIAN TRIBE;

    Intervenor-Plaintiffs,

    v.

STATE OF WASHINGTON,

    Defendant,

THOR C. TOLLEFSON, Director, Washington State Department of Fisheries; CARL CROUSE, Director, Washington Department of Game; and WASHINGTON STATE GAME COMMISSION; and WASHINGTON REEF NET OWNERS ASSOCIATION,

    Intervenor-Defendants

CIVIL NO. 9213

HON. GEORGE H. BOLDT
SENIOR UNITED STATES
DISTRICT JUDGE
PRESIDING

FINAL DECISION #I
Re All Issues
Submitted for
Decision 1/11/74

In <u>United States v. Washington</u>, Judge Boldt held that "all usual and accustomed grounds and stations" meant "every fishing location where members of a tribe customarily fished from time to time, at and before treaty time, however distant from the then usual habitat of the tribe, and whether or not other tribes then fished the same water..."

This access to off-reservation fishing areas is "in common with all citizens of the Territory" and must be shared with non-Indians. The state, however, cannot diminish the rights of the Indians nor can it regulate Indian fishing to the same degree it can non-Indian fishing. This is because the Indians have a federally-secured <u>right</u> to take fish, whereas other persons may take fish only to the extent that the state allows them to do so. Thus such other persons have only a privilege to take fish--a privilege which is dependent upon state authorization. Furthermore, where non-Indian fishing interferes with the fishing rights of treaty Indians, the non-Indian fishing must be curtailed or regulated in such a manner as to preserve the superior Indian rights.

Judge Boldt held that the Indians' treaty right was non-exclusive, that to fish "in common" with non-Indians means sharing equally on a 50-50 basis in the harvestable fish not needed for spawning escapement. He ruled, however, that fish taken by the Indians on their reservations – or off-reservation for subsistence or Indian ceremonial purposes – not be counted against the 50 per cent Indian share.

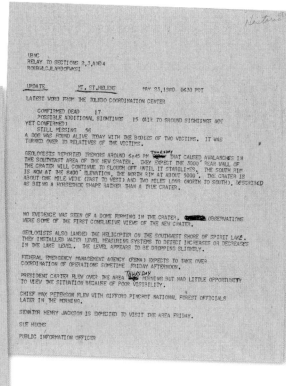

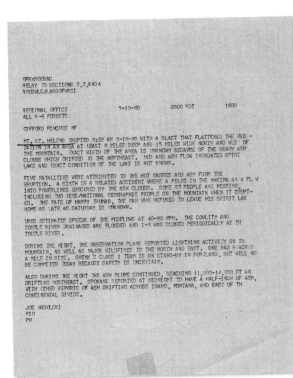

VANCOUVER, VANCOUVER! THIS IS IT!

On March 27, 1980, steam explosions blasted through Mount St. Helens's summit ice cap, and the new crater quickly grew to thirteen hundred feet in diameter. By the middle of May, more than ten thousand earthquakes had rippled through the volcano, and Mount St. Helens's northern flank bulged outward almost five hundred feet. On May 18, 1980, a magnitude 5.1 earthquake struck at 8:32 a.m., and the volcano's bulge and summit slid away in a huge landslide—the largest ever recorded on this planet. Powerful explosions ripped through the sliding debris, and a huge plume of volcanic gas and steam blasted up, rising fifteen miles in fifteen minutes. Less than an hour later, a second eruption took place. Just after noon, avalanches of hot ash, pumice, and gas roared out of the crater at more than fifty miles per hour. Water surged from melted snow, mixing with loose debris to form volcanic mudflows, or lahars, powerful enough to rip trees up by their roots. The most destructive lahar coursed down the path of the North Fork Toutle River, destroying bridges and homes and eventually flowing into the Cowlitz River. Over the course of the day, prevailing winds blew more than five hundred million tons of ash eastward, causing complete darkness in Spokane. Here are a few of the radio transcriptions and press releases from the National Forest Service office.

EASTSIDE, WESTSIDE

Eastern Washington and Western Washington are different from one another, and those differences can be heightened and caricatured. Western Washington can be seen as the "wetside," where it's always raining; Eastern Washington as an arid, sun-baked desert. Western Washingtonians can be seen as arrogant lounge lizards; Eastern Washingtonians as drawling rednecks. Western Washington is industrial; Eastern Washington is agricultural. These characterizations are exaggerated, but the realities of weather, terrain, and transportation have differentiated the two Washingtons, divided by the Cascade Curtain. Above, Shaw McCutcheon's political cartoon, which appeared in Spokane's *Spokesman-Review* on May 5, 1983, expressed the eastside perception that their interests are ignored by state legislators. Here, essential Eastern Washington projects have gone unfunded in Olympia—they've been left behind at the ferry landing. Meanwhile the ferry of State Bonding Capacity has been completely filled with $90 million to fund the convention center in downtown Seattle. That ferry has sailed.

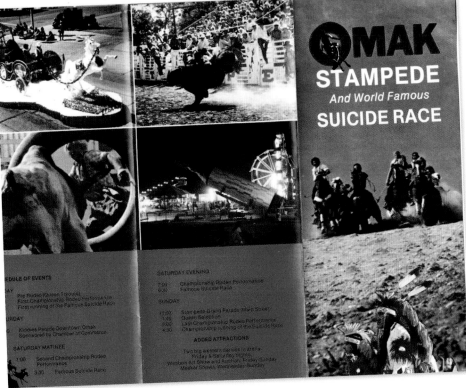

OMAK STAMPEDE

In 1933 two Okanogan County stockmen, Leo Moomaw and Tim Bernard, approached Omak's businessmen with the dream of a real live rodeo that would put the little town on the map. Native people had held mountain races for many years and in 1935, Omak Stampede planners added the Suicide Race to the rodeo; it soon became the Stampede's signature event. During the Suicide Race, riders start fifty feet back from the hill's edge, then plunge down the nearly vertical embankment and into the Okanogan River. Once their horses have crossed the river, the riders race up the bank and into the Stampede arena. Also, Native people had traditionally camped near Omak—in fact, much of the town is on the Colville Indian Reservation, and Stampede organizers encouraged the annual encampment at Stampede time, complete with dances, drumming, and stick games. The Stampede has not been without controversy, but today the Omak Stampede draws audiences of about twenty-five thousand to a week of events. This flyer, from the 1982 Omak Stampede, advertised the upcoming Fiftieth Anniversary Stampede.

THREE-CHORD ANTHEM

In 1955 Richard Berry wrote the calypso-style song "Louie Louie," about a lovesick Jamaican sailor, and the song was soon covered by the Wailers and others. The 1963 recording by the Portland band the Kingsmen was a hit and is the best-known version, characterized by its wild instrumental break and the incomprehensibility of its suggestive lyrics. At the time, the song was met with considerable outrage and banned on many radio stations. Eventually the Federal Bureau of Investigation reached the amusing conclusion that "Louie Louie" was not obscene because it was "unintelligible at any speed." Thanks in large part to Ross Shafer and the other cutups of KING-TV's *Almost Live*, "Louie Louie" almost became the official state song, to replace "Washington, My Home." Whatcom County commissioner Craig Cole brought Resolution No. 85-12 before the state legislature, citing the need for a "contemporary theme song that can be used to engender a sense of pride and community, and in the enhancement of tourism and economic development." In support of Cole's initiative, Shafer handed out sixty thousand "Louie Louie" pins and led a march on Olympia, where the bill was debated on the Senate floor. "Louie Louie" was never adopted as the state song, but Senate Resolution No. 85-37 declared April 12, 1985, to be Louie Louie Day, as you see in this flyer. Fans have called "Louie Louie" the first punk song and the bridge to hard rock, but the song has most significantly become Washington's "raunchy three-chord anthem," according to *Post-Intelligencer* reporter Gene Stout (June 22, 2000). Featured by the University of Washington marching band at football games and played at every Mariners game during the bottom of the seventh inning, "Louie Louie" is considered the state's unofficial rock song.

P U B L I C N O T I C E

The Washington State Senate Hereby Proclaims

♪ LOUIE LOUIE DAY ♪

April 12, 1985

New Washington lyrics to the legendary rock tune **"Louie Louie"** will be celebrated by Northwest bands and the public

Noon, April 12, 1985, Capitol Rotunda

Featuring:	**George Barner and the Trendsetters**
	Kingsmen
	Ferndale Orchestra
	Al Williams, Senator, Seattle
	Carl Cook, KGY Radio
	Craig Cole, Councilman, Whatcom County
	Ross Shafer, Host, "Almost Live"

. . . yeah, yeah, me gotta go!

860224 09

INTRODUCED BY: RON SIMS / BRUCE LAING

PROPOSED NO.: 86-66

MOTION NO. 6461

A MOTION setting forth the historical basis for "renaming" King County after the Reverend Dr. Martin Luther King, Jr., instead of William Rufus DeVane King for whom King County is currently named.

WHEREAS, the County of King in the State of Washington was named after William Rufus DeVane King by the Oregon Territorial legislature in 1852, and

WHEREAS, William Rufus DeVane King was a slaveowner and a 'gentle slave monger' according to John Quincy Adams, and

WHEREAS, the citizens of King County believe that the ownership of another human being is an injustice against humanity, and

WHEREAS, William Rufus DeVane King earned income and maintained his lifestyle by oppressing and exploiting other human beings, and

WHEREAS, the citizens of King County cherish and uphold the constitutional tenet of the 'unmitigated pursuit' of life, liberty, and happiness for which many citizens of this country have given their lives as a supreme sacrifice to defend these foundations of freedom, and

WHEREAS, the citizens of King County through their various faiths uphold the principle that all mankind was created equal, and

WHEREAS, Reverend Dr. Martin Luther King, Jr. believed that liberty, justice and freedom were the 'inalienable rights' of all men, women and children, and

WHEREAS, Reverend Dr. Martin Luther King, Jr. was a spiritual man who believed all people were created equal in the sight of God, and

WHEREAS, Reverend Dr. Martin Luther King, Jr. believed in the dignity and self-worth of every individual, and subsequently, gave his life defending his beliefs, and

---

6461

WHEREAS, Reverend Dr. Martin Luther King, Jr. a recipient of the Nobel Prize became a national hero whose birthday has been declared a national holiday by his nation's government to be a day of peace, love and understanding, and

WHEREAS, Reverend Dr. Martin Luther King, Jr. through his persistent and unfailing efforts prompted passage of the Civil Rights Act of 1964, and the Voting Rights Act of 1965, both of which have benefited all citizens of this nation, and

WHEREAS, Reverend Dr. Martin Luther King, Jr. inspired people and nations world-wide to strive in a non-violent manner for the human rights, civil liberties, and economic guarantees rightfully due people of all races;

NOW, THEREFORE, BE IT MOVED by the Council of King County: The King County Council, hereby, sets forth the historical basis for the "renaming" of King County in honor of Reverend Dr. Martin Luther King, Jr., a man whose contributions are well-documented and celebrated by millions throughout this nation and the world, and embody the attributes for which the citizens of King County can be proud, and claim as their own.

BE IT FURTHER MOVED,

King County shall be named after the Reverend Dr. Martin Luther King, Jr.

PASSED THIS 24th day of February, 1986.

KING COUNTY COUNCIL
KING COUNTY, WAHSINGTON

Audrey Gruger
Chair

ATTEST:

Dorothy M. Owens
Clerk of the Council

KING COUNTY

King County was first named to honor Alabaman William Rufus King, vice president under President Franklin Pierce when the county was originally formed in 1852 as part of Oregon Territory. Considered a moderate in his day on issues of race and slavery, King nevertheless ran on Pierce's pro-slavery ticket and was himself an extensive slaveholder. The Reverend Dr. Martin Luther King visited Seattle in the fall of 1961 and left a lasting impression; twenty-five years later, in 1986, black Democrat Ron Sims and white Republican Bruce Laing cosponsored legislation before the King County Council to honor Reverend King as the person for whom the county is named. In 2005, the state Legislature approved a bill adding Dr. King as the county's official namesake in state codes, which was signed into law by Governor Christine Gregoire. King County's name salutes the legacy of Reverend King, a Nobel Peace Prize winner, the nation's pre-eminent leader for civil rights, and an international icon of peace and justice.

131

The Challenge

The United States is embarking on an environmental cleanup effort that dwarfs any scientific enterprise this country has ever undertaken. Using available technology, the projected cost for cleaning up the tens of thousands of toxic waste sites across the nation, including the DOE sites, exceeds one trillion dollars, with no guarantee that the sites can be restored to their original condition and no consensus on "how clean is clean enough."

A significant portion of the nation's toxic waste generated over nearly 50 years of nuclear weapons research and production exists at Hanford. This 560-square-mile site contains one-third of all the inactive waste sites, one-half of the transuranic waste, and two-thirds of the high-level radioactive waste volume that exists across the entire DOE complex.

Many scientific problems related to the cleanup of these sites are unresolved and extremely complex, yet their solution is critical to our quality of life and economic competitiveness. The scientific community is being challenged to solve these problems and develop safer, more effective, less costly methods of cleaning up our air, land, and water. The EMSL will play a major role in meeting this challenge.

Major Cleanup Challenges at Hanford (metric tons)

Nuclear Material	6,900
Tank Waste	770,000
Contaminated Soil	125,000,000
Contaminated Groundwater	1,100,000,000
Solid Waste	400,000
Material from Facilities to be Decommissioned and Decontaminated	430,000

The Hanford site contains some of the DOE's most scientifically challenging waste cleanup problems:
- one-third of all DOE inactive waste sites
- one-half of DOE's transuranic waste
- two-thirds of DOE's high-level waste volume
- one-third of DOE's high-level waste radioactivity

EMSL research and technology development efforts will play a major role in meeting these challenges.

"...the scope and complexity of the contamination throughout the Weapons Complex present unprecedented challenges."

Complex Cleanup: The Environmental Legacy of Nuclear Weapons Production, Congress of the United States, Office of Technology Assessment, February 1991.

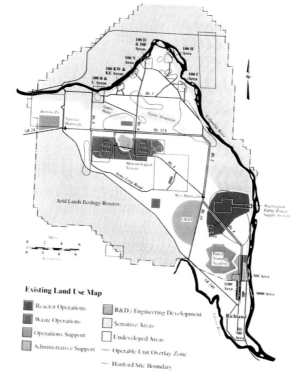

Existing Land Use Map

- Reactor Operations
- Waste Operations
- Operations Support
- Administrative Support
- R&D / Engineering Development
- Sensitive Areas
- Undeveloped Areas
- — Operable Unit Overlay Zone
- — Hanford Site Boundary

SORT OF FUZZING UP THE MESSAGE

NUCLEAR WASTE NOT WANTED!!

WHO WANTS NUCLEAR WASTE IN THEIR BACK YARD?

WASHINGTON STATE

NUCLEAR FILL WANTED HANFORD

WE DO!

TRI-CITIES

WASHINGTON

SHAW McCUTCHEON

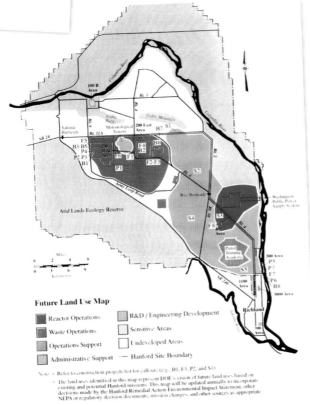

Future Land Use Map

- Reactor Operations
- Waste Operations
- Operations Support
- Administrative Support
- R&D / Engineering Development
- Sensitive Areas
- Undeveloped Areas
- — Hanford Site Boundary

Note: • Refer to construction projects list for callouts (e.g., B1, F3, P2, and S1)
• The land uses identified in this map represent DOE's vision of future land uses based on existing and potential Hanford missions. This map will be updated annually to incorporate decisions made by the Hanford Remedial Action Environmental Impact Statement, other NEPA or regulatory decision documents, mission changes, and other sources as appropriate.

Public Comments and Responses to the 1989 Hanford Cleanup Five-Year Plan

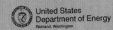

United States
Department of Energy
Richland, Washington

Approved for Public Release

COMMENT:

I don't trust anyone here today because you don't know things today that you'll know in forty more years. (The Dalles)

RESPONSE:

True. We all continue to learn. As we study sites and gain experience in cleanup, our knowledge will continue to increase. So will available technology. We will probably learn a great deal, and it is likely some of our current understandings will not stand the test of time. But we cannot stand still and do nothing, hoping our understanding will become complete somehow. It never will.

COMMENT:

I'm just furious you're talking about low-level radiation as if it's not a risk to our health. Are you aware of the BEIR-V report? While this stuff will be leaking into the Columbia, the lifeline of this whole area. (Portland) Do not discount the danger of low-level waste. (The Dalles, Portland)

RESPONSE:

We do not intend to imply that low-level radiation is not harmful. We are continuing to upgrade our waste management programs and have begun site cleanup because we are concerned with the legacy left by the last 45 years of operations.

Yes, managers and health physics people at Hanford are very aware of the BEIR-V report (NAS 1990). Since its release, and we continue to study it. Since its release, and partly in response to the report, we have lowered worker radiation exposure guidelines at Hanford.

COMMENT:

Decommissioning is a concern to the Yakima Indian Nation. Decommissioning is like leaving a high-level repository on the surface. (Yakima Indian Nation representative)

RESPONSE:

Decommissioning is not like leaving a high-level repository on the surface. It involves removing or containing contamination in old structures.

Decommissioning efforts are designed to remove contaminated materials from the accessible environment. Any residual contamination that could not be removed would be encapsulated in place to prevent migration.

We agree that decommissioning more than 100 old facilities at Hanford raises many concerns. We intend to work with the Indian nations, the States of Washington and Oregon, and the public as we address these concerns. The concerns include the tradeoffs of burying the contaminated materials at the current sites or disposing of them at new sites. This is the major issue being explored in the environmental impact statement for the decommissioning of the old production reactors.

2.29 VITRIFICATION

COMMENT:

Has vitrification been demonstrated?

RESPONSE:

Yes. Since the 1950's, extensive research and developmental efforts in the United States and elsewhere have established the viability of vitrification for producing the borosilicate glass waste form.

COMMENT:

How is decommissioning done? (Walla Walla)

RESPONSE:

Reactors at Hanford can be decommissioned a number of ways. Options range from leaving them in place and covering them with a protective barrier, to removing them completely and cleaning up the contamination. Removal options being considered include immediate one-piece transport of the reactor structure to a higher elevation near the center of the site, or waiting for many years and then disassembling the structure for disposal as low-level waste. Most of the radioactivity is low-level and is the kind that will have to stay at Hanford. The final environmental impact statement for the surplus reactors at Hanford is due to be released soon. This environmental impact statement will be used to evaluate the options for decommissioning the eight surplus Hanford reactors.

COMMENT:

If you leave them intact, what kind of radiation will they be putting into the air? (Walla Walla)

RESPONSE:

If the old reactors were left intact we would take actions to prevent release of radioactivity to the environment above regulatory limits. This would be followed by appropriate surveillance and maintenance to insure that larger releases do not occur.

COMMENT:

In about 1971, I attended a meeting by Battelle at which they assured us point blank there was _no_ possibility that contamination from Hanford Site could leach into or otherwise reach the Columbia. Not a small possibility, _no_ possibility. Then later, almost immediately after a leak at Hanford was announced, the water monitoring at Bonneville Dam was canceled (my father worked there). (Bellevue)

RESPONSE:

If someone said this in 1971, he or she was wrong. We are sorry. Some amounts of contamination continue to enter the Columbia River even now.

HANFORD CLEAN-UP

By the end of the Cold War, the Hanford Nuclear Reservation housed nine nuclear reactors and five plutonium processing plants, and had armed most of the nuclear weapons in the U.S. arsenal. Safety procedures to manage radioactive waste proved inadequate, and Hanford operations had released significant amounts of radioactive material into the air, the ground, and the Columbia River. After 1977 the Department of Energy (DOE) took over responsibility for Hanford, declared the most contaminated nuclear site in the United States. Today Hanford includes the Columbia Generating Station, a nuclear power plant, as well as scientific laboratories, but Hanford also houses the nation's largest and most sophisticated environmental cleanup initiative. On May 15, 1989, the state Department of Ecology, the Environmental Protection Agency, and the DOE entered an agreement to restore the Columbia River and develop a long-term waste treatment and storage facility for more than fifty million gallons of radioactive and chemical waste. Here you see historic material from the 1980s that documents the Hanford challenge, the plans, public comment, and—finally—the opportunity. First, a marked-up statement of the challenge and two maps of the Hanford site, one from the mid-1980s and the second from an imagined future; then sets of frank comments from area stakeholders, ranging from tribal members to ordinary citizens, and the responses. Finally, Shaw McCutcheon's political cartoon, published February 26, 1985, in the *Spokesman-Review*, pithily pokes fun at the Tri-Cities' opportunism.

NOV. • Washington •
100 YRS
Centennial Celebration •

Celebrate
WASHINGTON • CENTENNIAL 89

WASHINGTON'S CENTENNIAL

In 1989 Washington State commemorated its one-hundredth birthday, and many years of planning culminated in a year of special events, from fireworks displays to exhibitions. The Washington Centennial Commission was charged with marking three significant anniversaries: the 1987 bicentennial of the U.S. Constitution, the 1992 bicentennial of the Pacific Northwest voyages of Robert Gray and George Vancouver, and the sesquicentennial of Charles Wilkes's naval expedition; plus the celebration of Washington's 1889 admission as a state. To celebrate the centennial of statehood, the commission planned a range of programs to engage as many Washingtonians as possible. For instance, the Washington State History Museum offered the Centennial Hall of Honor exhibition. A new state park, Centennial Trail Park, was opened near Spokane. The new azalea cultivar named "Washington State Centennial" was brought to market.

A full-size replica of the sloop *Lady Washington* was launched at Aberdeen to commemorate the voyage of American Robert Gray, who named the Columbia River in 1792. A number of commemorative items were available, including a special edition Winchester rifle, ceramics, cookbooks, lapel pins, stamps, posters, token coins, and much more. For Native people, the centennial was bittersweet, and a new accord was signed in 1989 between Washington's federally recognized tribes and the Governor's Office of Indian Affairs. In 1989, too, the first multitribal paddle in many years took place, the Paddle to Seattle, from Suquamish, initiating the enduring tradition of Tribal Journeys. Here you see an image of the winning design for the centennial license plate, and the centennial logo from the periodical *Celebrate!* published by the Washington Centennial Commission.

SUB POP GRUNGE

This is the poster for Sub Pop's first Lame Fest (June 9, 1989), featuring Mudhoney, Tad, and Nirvana. Sub Pop began life as a fanzine entitled *Subterranean Pop*, created by Bruce Pavitt for course credit while enrolled at Evergreen State College. In 1983 Pavitt left Evergreen behind and moved north to Seattle; three years later he released the first Sub Pop compilation cassette, which featured material from local bands. Jonathan Poneman joined Sub Pop in 1987, and the following year both Poneman and Pavitt quit their day jobs to incorporate Sub Pop. That summer, defining the "Seattle Sound," Sub Pop released the first Mudhoney single, "Touch Me I'm Sick," and then the first Nirvana single, "Love Buzz." Early Sub Pop was as much a fan club as a record label, booking subscribers in the Sub Pop Singles Club that distributed singles by mail—in 1990 the club had two thousand members. Sub Pop staged a party for the fans in June 1989: the Lame Fest at Seattle's venerable Moore Theatre. Nirvana was the opening act, and the kids packed the house for the Seattle Sound, or "grunge." Gillian Gaar, in *Seattle Weekly*, October 26, 2009, reported that Nirvana drummer Chad Channing happily remembers that in 1989, the show's poster—presumably this one—was the biggest one he'd ever seen the band's name on.

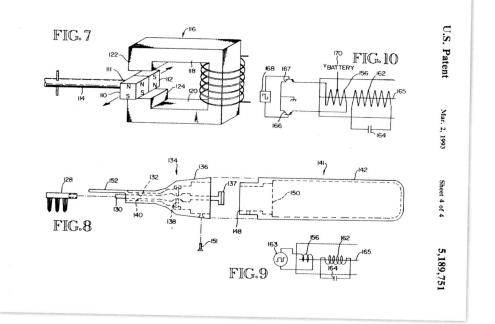

United States Patent [19]
Giuliani et al.

[11] Patent Number: 5,189,751
[45] Date of Patent: Mar. 2, 1993

[54] VIBRATING TOOTHBRUSH USING A MAGNETIC DRIVER

[75] Inventors: David Giuliani, Mercer Island; Roy W. Martin, Redmond; Rodger H. Rosenbaum, Seattle, all of Wash.

[73] Assignee: Gemtech, Inc., Mercer Island, Wash.

[21] Appl. No.: 672,844

[22] Filed: Mar. 21, 1991

[51] Int. Cl.⁵ A61C 17/34; B08B 13/02
[52] U.S. Cl. 15/22.1; 310/36
[58] Field of Search 15/22.1, 22.2, 22.4; 310/10, 20, 27, 36, 37, 39, 464/29

[56] References Cited

U.S. PATENT DOCUMENTS

1,832,519	11/1931	Wheat et al.	15/22.1
2,044,863	6/1936	Sticht	15/22.1
2,246,523	6/1941	Kulik	15/22.1
2,278,365	3/1942	Daniels	15/22.1
2,709,227	5/1955	Foley et al.	310/29
2,734,139	2/1956	Murphy	15/22.1
2,878,499	3/1959	Pressman	15/22.1
2,917,758	12/1959	Held	15/22.1
2,977,614	4/1961	Demanuele	15/22.1
3,159,859	12/1964	Rasmussen	15/22.1
3,493,793	2/1970	Niemela	310/37
3,500,080	2/1970	Bey	310/36
3,535,726	10/1970	Sawyer	15/22.1
3,538,359	11/1970	Barowski	15/22.1
4,787,847	11/1988	Martin et al.	15/22.2

FOREIGN PATENT DOCUMENTS

609238 2/1979 Switzerland 15/22.1

Primary Examiner—Edward L. Roberts

[57] ABSTRACT

A vibrating toothbrush which includes a toothbrush body (12) and a lever arm (14) having toothbrush bristles (18) at one end thereof. The lever arm (14) is mounted for pivotal movement at a pivot member (16) which is in the vicinity of the other end of the lever arm (14). In one embodiment, a pair of permanent magnets (44, 46) are provided at the other end of the lever arm (14), positioned side-by-side with opposite polarities. An electromagnet (24) is provided to the rear of the lever arm (14). The electromagnet (24) includes an E-core having top, bottom and center legs (30, 31, 33) with a coil (36) wound around its center leg (33) which receives an alternating current driving signal from an oscillator/battery section (38). The frequency of operation is in the range of 150–400 Hz. The action of the alternating current in the electromagnet (24) causes the lever arm (14) to move about the pivot member (16), first in one direction and then in an opposing direction to provide the desired vibrating effect.

51 Claims, 4 Drawing Sheets

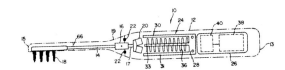

INTELLECTUAL PROPERTY

The United States Patent Office is a treasure trove for the exploration of creativity and innovation. In 1987 University of Washington professors David Engel and Roy Martin met with engineer David Giuliani, and the three entrepreneurs ultimately formed the startup Gemtech, with funding from twenty-five local investors. After several years of research and prototyping, the Sonicare toothbrush was introduced at a periodontal conference in November 1992, and this patent was issued the following year. Here you see the drawings and some of the documentation offered to the patent office by Gemtech of Mercer Island, Washington, for Patent No. 5,189,752, the "Vibrating Toothbrush Using a Magnetic Driver" that we consumers know as the Sonicare toothbrush. After reviewing the prior art in the field, the patent disclosed the invention and set out its claims. Two years later, Gemtech became Optiva Corporation, named in 1997 by *Inc.* magazine as the country's fastest-growing privately held company. Philips Electronics North America acquired Optiva in 2000. By the end of 2001, Sonicare had become the number-one selling rechargeable power toothbrush in the United States. Today more than seven million Sonicare toothbrushes have been sold worldwide.

GAY PRIDE

In June 1974 Seattle's lesbians and gays celebrated the city's first Gay Pride Week, to mark the fifth anniversary of a 1969 New York City police raid on the Stonewall Inn in Greenwich Village, resisted by gay and lesbian customers. Their resistance became a rallying for the gay rights movement, to come out from the closet and the shadows with pride. By the time of the poster shown here, 1995, Seattle Pride had become an annual celebration for gay, lesbian, bisexual, and transgendered people and their friends. The poster's motifs incorporated the rainbow, one of the most widely recognized symbols of gay pride, in the framing of the iconic Space Needle. The triangle itself reminds us of the heritage of persecution of gay people, in which gay prisoners sent to Nazi concentration camps were required to wear a pink downward-pointing triangle on their shirts. Design of the gay rainbow is attributed to artist Gilbert Becker, who devised the flag in which red represents life; orange, healing; yellow, the sun; green, nature; blue, art; indigo, harmony; and violet, the spirit. Echoing Frederick Douglass, the poster boldly proclaimed, "No one is free until all are free." At the bottom of the triangle is the Greek letter lambda, a longstanding symbol of solidarity within the gay community. The poster also articulated the gay action agenda, some of which has been accomplished. On June 29, 1974, the *Seattle Post-Intelligencer* reported that about two hundred attended that first Gay Pride event. In 2010 more than seventy thousand turned out for Seattle Pride and Pridefest.

PEAK EXPERIENCE

Westsiders orient themselves by Mount Rainier—on clear days they say, "The mountain is out," and stare at its tremendous mass and glory in its presence. Here, on July 27, 1993, these climbers had made it to the top, and stood on the summit of the mountain, exhausted and ecstatic. They described their route, their experience, and their climbing teams in this weathered green record book. At 14,410 feet above sea level, at the top of the world on a cloudless day, their view was stupendous. One couple celebrated their twentieth wedding anniversary on the peak. Another climber logged his seventh summit—the first when he was twenty, this one when he was fifty. He ruefully noted that the climb didn't get easier with age. A second climber described the trek as hellacious but worth it. Readers who remember the controversy over Mount Rainier's name will smile at seeing climbers refer to the peak as Tahoma. And some just wrote, "I made it!"

7/27/93 Thank you Tahoma. Couldn't have done it w/o you Gretch - once again. This is better than Kilimanjaro! What an insane climbing group and friends.
Tara Lesley Pickens

7/27/93 Elated to be here on Tahoma, 4th summit, but the first by this route (Schurman/Emmons). It's an unusually spectacular day, & ever so great to be here w/friends — trusty roomate Matt, crazy Shodan John, my hero nidan Jerry, +, most of all, to my best friend, who is always part of my rope team.
Bless Tahoma, Shotokan Karate, & Life!
— Gretchen E. Manton

7/27/93 What a gorgeous day!! After a month of waiting, a window of good weather. It's worth the wait! The stars were incredible, the dawn beautiful, the day tremendous. I see my insignificance and the beauty of nature + life!
Sheila Doppelhammer

I second what Sheila just said. This is my 5th (?) climb of Rainier, the first when I was 20 and the last (today) when I was 50. Tahoma doesn't get any easier with age!
Steven Hodge

7-27-93 Bob Fusendin
FINALLY TO THE TOP ON TRY TWO. BEAUTIFUL!

7/27/93 Bill Armstrong - Woburn, mass Ma, Stephen Duclos Boston, Ma, Dan McCann, Boxford, Ma. Emmons Route. A super fine day. Thank you Mother Mountain

7/27/93
Exactly 20 years ago we were wed on the true summit of Rainier — the first to our knowledge. This is our anniversary climb — The summit is still as windy! Ingraham Direct route this time — Kautz route last 20 years ago.
Diane La Course
& Ron Jackson

27 July 93 Jerry Bentley with the help of good friends once again.

7/27/93 John Gosink A hellacious trip up, but man what a beautiful view

WINDOWS 95

On August 24, 1995, a huge circus tent was set up on the Microsoft campus in Redmond, and Jay Leno acted as master of ceremonies while Bill Gates launched Windows 95 for the crowd. It was a festive day, with a Ferris wheel, rock bands, and picnic food galore. While the Rolling Stones' "Start Me Up" played, the focus was on Windows 95's easy-to-use "Start" button. Driven by an intense media blitz, consumers had lined up overnight outside stores, eager to buy Microsoft's intuitive, user-friendly product, a departure from the forbidding DOS command line. Similarities between Windows 95 and the Apple Macintosh's look and feel led to years of bitter litigation between Microsoft and Apple. Within two years of release, Windows 95 had gained huge market share and became the most successful operating system ever produced. The new product was originally shipped without Internet Explorer, Microsoft's web browser, but you see it featured prominently here: "The Internet Explorer Starter Kit NOW included INSIDE!" The Windows 95 distinctive start menu and task bar set the style for computer screens at work and at home, all around the world, and Windows 95 was the ancestor of the Microsoft software that followed, including Windows 98, Windows NT, Windows 2000, Windows Vista, and Windows 7. In the mid-1990s, Microsoft became the company that best represented metro Seattle's sense of itself heading into the twenty-first century—a livable, diverse, well-educated, innovative, international city.

WAR

LOW WAGES

DEFORESTATION

GENTRIFICATION

GRIDLOCKED CITIES

GENETIC ENGINEERING

THE RICH GETTING RICHER

CUTS IN SOCIAL SERVICES

INCREASING POVERTY

MEANINGLESS JOBS

GLOBAL WARMING

MORE PRISONS

SWEATSHOPS

BATTLE IN SEATTLE

Between November 29 and December 3, 1999, the World Trade Organization Ministerial Conference convened in Seattle to debate and develop global trade policies. Opponents of these World Trade Organization (WTO) policies saw them as cynical and exploitive efforts by developed, first-world countries to advance a worldwide corporate agenda. Demonstrators gathered in Seattle to engage in protests that ranged from peaceful assembly to vandalism and violence. This Direct Action Network poster graphically illustrates the way that protestors perceived the WTO and the results of its trade policies, as well as their intent to shut down the conference. Well-organized protests brought Seattle to a standstill and halted the WTO, confining delegates to their hotels. As the mayhem escalated, Mayor Paul Schell declared a state of emergency, and riot gear–equipped police fought protestors with tear gas, pepper spray, rubber bullets, and mass arrests. An astonished worldwide audience watched television coverage of the Battle in Seattle. By the end, six hundred protestors were in jail, and parts of the city looked like war zones.

VOX POPULI

After a long campaign, Washington State voters ratified the constitutional amendment for the initiative and referendum in 1912 that authorized the right of public petition to place a measure on the ballot. This progressive reform put legislative authority firmly in the hands of the people, and was intended to limit legislative control by powerful special interests. In 1999 political outsider Timothy Eyman and a small army of volunteers gathered more than five hundred thousand signatures to qualify initiative I-695 for the November ballot. Widely known as the "$30 License Tab Initiative," I-695 tapped deep frustration with the motor vehicle excise tax—2.2 percent of the vehicle's value—and called for reducing annual license tab renewals to a flat rate of thirty dollars. On November 2, 1999, I-695 passed with fifty-six percent of the popular vote, though few voters may have realized that they were voting for sweeping controls on their government's capacity to raise money, requiring voter approval to increase taxes, fees, and any other "monetary charge." Responding to the unpopularity of the excise tax, the 1999 state legislature voted almost immediately to eliminate it, mandating the flat thirty-dollar license tab fee. Overnight, predicted state revenue fell seven percent. The loss of $750 million per year drove the legislature in Olympia into a long special session, where legislators were unable to agree on the necessary budget reductions. Fearing deep cuts to service, transit workers, ferry riders, and municipal governments challenged I-695 in court even as then–Attorney General Christine Gregoire found, "We believe I-695 is constitutional and have taken the first steps to defend the initiative on behalf of the State of Washington." Three months later, King County Superior Court struck down as unconstitutional the section of the initiative requiring voter approval of any "monetary charge" by state government. Then, on October 26, 2000, a majority on the Washington State Supreme Court declared I-695 in violation of the state constitution and its language misleading to voters. At the time, Eyman made it clear that he would be back with new initiatives, and he has done so. "We think the only way voters in the state of Washington will get tax relief," he said, "is to vote for it." Here you see a pro-Initiative 695 flyer and an anti-Initiative 695 bumper sticker.

LET'S RAISE A GLASS

Since 1946 *Good Fruit Grower* has been published in Yakima, Washington, as a special interest periodical for Eastern Washington orchardists growing apricots, cherries, peaches, pears, plums, and apples. Though grapes were grown before World War I throughout the Yakima Valley, they comprised a very tiny part of Washington's fruit production. The first commercial-scale plantings of wine grapes began in the 1960s, and expansion was rapid throughout the 1970s and 1980s. But the 1990s were the decade of the "merlot craze," which swept the consumer market. Plantings of the merlot varietal increased more than fivefold during the 1990s, and Washington merlot wines were soon featured prominently in restaurants across the country. In 2000—the year that *Good Fruit Grower* ran this beautiful photo of merlot grapes on its cover—about twenty-six thousand acres in Washington State were devoted to viniferous grapes, and for the first time more red grapes were harvested in Washington than white. This photo was taken just before harvest, after a hard freeze had turned the grape leaves from green to red. The image also marks an agricultural revolution in Washington: In 1938 there were 42 wineries in the state; in 2000, when this photo ran, there were 163. Today there are more than six hundred wineries in the state, and wine has become a $3 billion business.

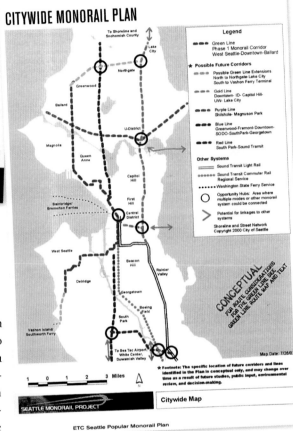

CITYWIDE MONORAIL PLAN

Citywide Map

ETC Seattle Popular Monorail Plan

1962 MODEL TECHNOLOGY IN 2005 SEATTLE

The Alweg Monorail was a model technology at the 1962 World's Fair, connecting the fairgrounds with downtown Seattle at the Westlake station. A demonstration of single-rail, high-speed public transportation, the monorail seemed to point the way to the future. In the Washington State Pavilion, visitors marveled at a huge model of central Puget Sound in the twenty-first century, threaded by hundreds of miles of monorail, and the fair's program included a euphoric description of the monorail experience: "The two slim white rails, narrowing in unison toward infinity, skim over the noise and the clutter of street traffic . . . and ahead is the straightaway—a mile of unswerving concrete beam. The driver accelerates. . . . Twenty miles per hour . . . forty . . . sixty . . . seventy. . . . The driver decelerates and . . . the monorail train eases over the crowds and across the fence and slips into Century 21 Station. One hundred twenty-five persons rise from their seats and step out to enjoy

the Seattle World's Fair. The elapsed time from downtown—ninety-five seconds." Fast-forward to the twenty-first century and ambitious plans for a citywide monorail plan in Seattle. Monorail enthusiasts hoped to accomplish the 1962 dream, and in 2002 the citizens of Seattle voted to authorize construction of the fourteen-mile Green Line. Three years later the Seattle Popular Monorail Authority negotiated a contract for construction of the Green Line, but the community balked at the financing plan that called for taxes until 2050 and required $9 billion in interest. On June 30, 2005, the Seattle Monorail Project board killed the system's financing and proposed a shorter version of the Green Line, cutting short its extension to West Seattle and to Ballard. However, in November 2005, Seattle citizens voted against construction of this shortened Green Line. Despite occasional glitches, the Alweg Monorail has continued its Seattle service, completing its millionth mile in 2008.

Born in Bothell, Washington, Patty Murray is one of seven siblings. She was educated in Bothell's public schools and received her B.A. degree from Washington State University in 1972. She met her husband Rob at WSU and they have been married for 26 years and have two children, Randy, 22, and Sara, 18.

Patty was an educator in Shoreline, a school board member and parent volunteer, and a State Senator before being elected to the U.S. Senate in 1992.

For more information or to volunteer, please visit our web site or call: www.pattymurray98.com
206-443-8636

U.S. Senator Patty Murray
Working Effectively for Us.

People for Patty Murray
P.O. Box 3662
Seattle, WA 98124

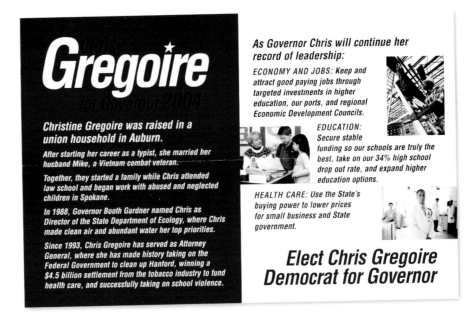

Gregoire
for Governor 2004

Christine Gregoire was raised in a union household in Auburn.

After starting her career as a typist, she married her husband Mike, a Vietnam combat veteran.

Together, they started a family while Chris attended law school and began work with abused and neglected children in Spokane.

In 1988, Governor Booth Gardner named Chris as Director of the State Department of Ecology, where Chris made clean air and abundant water her top priorities.

Since 1993, Chris Gregoire has served as Attorney General, where she has made history taking on the Federal Government to clean up Hanford, winning a $4.5 billion settlement from the tobacco industry to fund health care, and successfully taking on school violence.

As Governor Chris will continue her record of leadership:

ECONOMY AND JOBS: Keep and attract good paying jobs through targeted investments in higher education, our ports, and regional Economic Development Councils.

EDUCATION: Secure stable funding so our schools are truly the best, take on our 34% high school drop out rate, and expand higher education options.

HEALTH CARE: Use the State's buying power to lower prices for small business and State government.

Elect Chris Gregoire
Democrat for Governor

GEORGE Nethercutt
U.S. SENATE

Dino ROSSI
FOR GOVERNOR ■ GOP
www.dinorossi.com

GET OUT THE VOTE!

This anthology has set out hundreds of documents that range through the history of Washington Territory and State, 1853 to 2003. Here is some political ephemera from the 2004 election, which saw very high voter turnout across the state as President George W. Bush ran for reelection against Democrat John Kerry. Though Kerry won a majority of the vote in Washington, a review of the county-by-county voting clearly shows where his strength was and was not, in the Republican/Democrat, rural/urban division of the state, which remains to a large degree an eastern/western division. Patty Murray easily defended her U.S. Senate seat against Republican challenger George Nethercutt, though the distribution of the vote shows the same political divide. Gary Locke declined to run for a third term, and Christine Gregoire, state attorney general for eleven years, ran for governor in 2004 against Dino Rossi. Gregoire was eventually declared the winner after an extremely close race and two recounts. Governor Gregoire is Washington's second female governor, following Dixy Lee Ray, who governed the state from 1977 to 1981. Washington territorial and state politics have infused this long story of social, cultural, and economic history.

HOME

And here we see Washington State from space. The Landsat 7 was launched in 1999, more than ten years ago, to build a globally accessible archive of satellite photos of Earth. The satellite was programmed to circle the globe on a polar orbit, synchronized to the sun, and to "cover" our whole planet every sixteen days. This photograph of Washington is really a mosaic compiled from a set of digital images, shot over time from 500 miles above the earth. Linda Jonescheit, a technical specialist who works with these images at NASA, wrote me to explain that this "orthorectified" image is comprised of many photographs, "processed with panchromatic sharpening . . . [and] radiometrically matched and merged with corresponding Digital Elevation Model data." This miraculous technology has generated hundreds of cloud-free, crystal-clear images, archived by the United States Geological Survey, and made freely available on the Web for us to learn about our dynamic planet.

So here is Washington State, from a unique perspective. Look at it, this place of great character—the mountains and the drylands, the rivers and shorelines, the islands and valleys. You can pinpoint where you live, you can trace a car trip or a ferry ride. Follow the Columbia River, cross Snoqualmie Pass, find Mount Rainier. Rugged and fragile, filled with stories, Washington is our home. This place has been the setting for the shared experience documented in this book, as Washington people have dreamed and fought and worked, lived and died, leaving us their records to know them, as we shall one day be known.

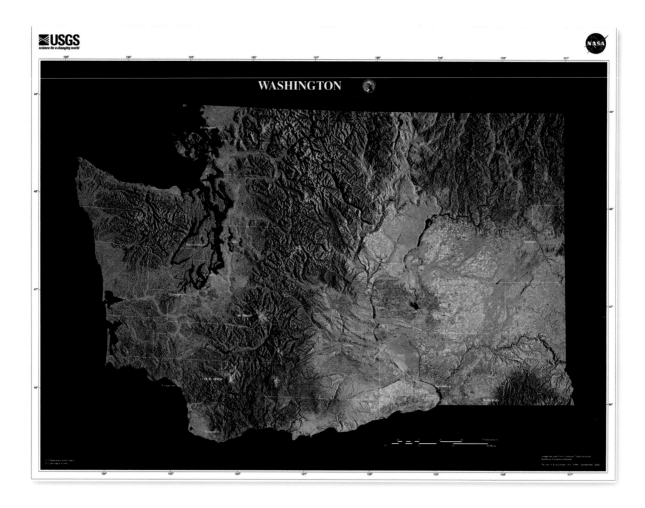

Citations

1. *Columbian*, Washington State Digital Archives www.digitalarchives.wa.gov/; seal and resolution, An Act to Adopt the Seal of the Territory of Washington, Laws of Washington Territory, 1854, and H.R. 348, An Act to Establish the Territorial Government of Washington, 1853, National Archives Microcopy #26, Roll 1, Washington State Archives, Olympia.

2. 2005.0.21.38, Washington State Historical Society.

3. Series 95, Record of Marriage Certificates 1853–1928, Book ½ A, King County Archives.

4–5. Point Elliott Treaty, 1855, Indian Treaties, General Records of the United States Government (Record Group [RG] 11), National Archives at Washington, DC. The National Archives in Seattle can provide a digital copy of this treaty; email seattle.archives@nara.gov.

6. 1932.93.16, Washington State Historical Society.

7. 2011.0.1, Stevens Manuscript Collection, Washington State Historical Society.

8–9. Thomas Stowell Phelps, *Reminiscences of Seattle: Washington Territory and the U. S. Sloop-of-War Decatur During the Indian War of 1855–56*, Seattle: The Alice Harriman Company. 1908; Militia and Longmire documents, Washington Territorial Volunteers Papers, 1855–56, Washington State Archives, Olympia.

10. *San Francisco Daily Evening Bulletin* online, "Nineteenth Century U.S. Newspapers" database at many public libraries; Douglas to Gholson, National Archives Microcopy #26, Roll 1, Washington State Archives, Olympia.

11. Tilton to McGill, National Archives Microcopy #26, Roll 1, Washington State Archives, Olympia.

12. Gholson to Black, National Archives Microcopy #26, Roll 1, Washington State Archives, Olympia.

13. 2006.0.507, Washington State Historical Society; *Walla Walla Statesman*, Washington State Digital Archives.

14. Pickering to Lincoln, September 8, 1864, Series I, General Correspondence, 1833–1916, The Abraham Lincoln Papers at the Library of Congress, accessible American Memory Project, www.loc.gov; Lincoln to Pickering, September 8, 1864, Vol. 1A, March 10–Oct. 11, 1864, Telegrams Sent By the President—Telegrams Sent and Received By the War Department, 1861–82 (Bound), Records of the Office of the Secretary of the Secretary of War, (RG 107), National Archives Building, Washington, DC.

15. UW18848, University of Washington Libraries, Special Collections.

16. 2009.54.1.4.13; 2009.54.1.4.16; 2009.54.1.4.17, Washington State Historical Society.

17. Probate Case Files, Thurston County Clerk, Washington State Archives, Olympia.

18. Patient Ledger, 1877–1897, RG 56, Providence Seattle Medical Center Collection, Providence Archives.

19. Series 320, Commissioners' Road Books 1854–1900, Book 4, page 21, Lake Washington and Cedar River Road (1877), King County Archives.

20. 1997.15, Washington State Historical Society.

21. Seattle Public Library, Special Collections.

22–23. Chinese businesses burned, UW 29392z, Watson Squire Papers, University of Washington Libraries, Special Collections; Yesler threat, UW29395z, Clarence Bagley Papers, University of Washington Libraries, Special Collections; *Seattle Daily Call* microfilm, University of Washington Libraries; illustration, 2002.3.410, Museum of History & Industry.

24–25. Seattle Public Library, Special Collections.

26. Washington Territorial Census Rolls, Walla Walla County, 1887, Washington State Archives, Olympia.

27. Washington Territorial Supreme Court, Case Files, 1888, Washington State Archives, Olympia.

28. Statehood, Elisha P. Ferry Papers, 1889, Washington State Archives, Olympia.

29. Lantern slide, 2002.3.135, Museum of History & Industry; Spokane and Ellensburgh articles, July 5, 1889 and August 5, 1889, *Seattle Times* microfilm; Seattle article, June 7, 1889, *Post-Intelligencer* microfilm.

30. Dan Boone and family, 2002-850-831, Yakima Valley Libraries.

31. Rules and Regulations, Minutes of the Meetings of the Washington State Board of Education, 1891, Washington State Archives, Olympia.

32. 72-9-81, Wold Collection, Issaquah Historical Society.

33. Immigration, John Rogers Papers, Washington State Archives, Olympia.

34. *Seattle Times* microfilm, University of Washington Libraries.

35. Application for Master's License, Bureau of Marine Inspection and Navigation (RG 41), National Archives at Seattle.

36. X.3472.822, Whatcom Museum, Bellingham.

37. 1994.4.123, Washington State Historical Society.

38. King County Clerk Probate Case Files, Washington State Archives—Puget Sound Branch.

39. Trademarks, 1902–03, Washington Secretary of State, Corporations Division, Washington State Archives, Olympia.

40. Shot from the hard copy *Seattle Times*, May 7, 1905.

41. MsSc 162, Washington State Historical Society.

42. MsSc 194, Northwest Museum of Arts and Culture.

43. Accession Number 008-0807, Washington State Digital Archives, A.M. Kendrick Photographic Collection, ca. 1890–1976. Imaged and indexed by Washington State Archives—Eastern Region, where original prints and negatives are housed.

44. Monte Cristo map, Series NW331-2-16B, Snohomish County Plat Maps, Washington State Archives—Northwest Region; Monte Cristo Railway, August 15, 1897, *Everett News*; Telluride, *Seattle Times*, August 17, 1900; Everett directories and *Everett News*, Northwest History Room, Everett Public Library.

45. Series 433, Marriage Returns 1891–1947, King County Archives.

46. Okanogan County Historical Society.

47. Northwest History Room, Everett Public Library.

48. Cowlitz County Historical Society.

49. Museum of History & Industry.

50. May Arkwright Hutton Collection, Northwest Museum of Arts and Culture.

51. 1910 U.S. census available Ancestry or Heritage Quest database, most public libraries; Everett city directories and *Everett Herald*, Northwest History Room, Everett Public Library; Boyer's "splendid business," October 17, 1902, her Forum presentation, April 12, 1907, *Seattle Republican*, digitized at Chronicling America, Library of Congress, http://chroniclingamerica.loc.gov/.

52. Spokane County Auditor, Marriage Certificates. Certificate A16087, Washington State Archives—Eastern Region.

53. Florine Alexander Collection, Eastside Heritage Center.

54–55. Alaska-Yukon-Pacific Exposition, General Postcard Collection, Washington State Archives; Pay Streak, shot from hard copy, May 7, 1905, *Seattle Times*; guide, map and ticket, 2006.3, Museum of History & Industry.

56. Song book, MS 68 1/24; WCTU program, MS 68 2/18, Northwest Museum of Arts and Culture.

57. Yakima Valley Museum.

58. Pend Oreille County Historical Society.

59. Swedish-Finn Historical Society.

60. Secret Service Reports, 1917, Ernest Lister Papers, Washington State Archives, Olympia.

61. Artificial History Files, Mount Rainier National Park, Records of the National Park Service (RG 79), National Archives at Seattle.

62. Cowlitz County Historical Society.

63. 94.7.256, Issaquah Historical Society.

64–65. Tacoma Public Library, http://search.tacomapubliclibrary.org/postcard.

66. Office of the City Clerk Ordinances, 1801–02, Seattle Municipal Archives.

67. 2002.28, Margaret Hardin Collection, Black Heritage Society of Washington State.

68–69. Capitalist Pyramid, UW 1535, University of Washington Libraries, Special Collections; IWW Membership Card and Songbook, Centralia Massacre Special Collection, Washington State Archives, Olympia; Letter to Governor Lister and Defense Notice, Labor—Everett Massacre, Ernest Lister Papers, Washington State Archives, Olympia; booking photos, Northwest Room, Everett Public Library.

70. PO-3050, White River Valley Museum, Auburn.

71. Artificial History Files, Mount Rainier National Park, Records of the National Park Service (RG 79), National Archives at Seattle.

72. July 21, 1923 and August 4, 1923, *Watcher on the Tower*; July 25 and August 1, 1924, *Issaquah Press*, both microfilm, University of Washington Libraries.

73. 96.24.01, Rainier Valley Historical Society.

74. 2004-114-408, Yakima Valley Museum, *Yakima Memory* http://yakimamemory.org.

75. Log Brand Registrations, Department of Natural Resources, Washington State Archives, Olympia.

76. Highway Department, Cascade Tunnel, 1925–33, Roland Hartley Papers, Washington State Archives, Olympia.

77. 1991.100.533, Wing Luke Museum of the Asian Pacific Experience.

78. Trademarks, 1925–29, Washington Secretary of State, Corporations Division, Washington State Archives, Olympia.

79. Flyer, Spokane County Prosecuting Attorney, Correspondence. Box 1, folder 29, Washington State Archives—Eastern Region; Poem, Washington Emergency Relief Administration, Roland Hartley Papers, Washington State Archives, Olympia.

80. 1967.137.13, R.D. Ginther Collection, Washington State Historical Society.

81. King County Assessor Real Property Record Cards, Washington State Archives—Puget Sound Branch.

82. Records Relating to Civilian Conservation Corps Activities, Mount Rainier National Park, Records of the National Park Service (RG 79), National Archives at Seattle.

83. Art_N779Pe06, Northwest Art Collection, Seattle Public Library, www.spl.org.

84. The Shafer Museum, Winthrop.

85. Grand Coulee Dam, Columbia Basin Commission and M.W.A.K. *Columbian* (1935–1941), CE867-8-3 ESD 171, Grand Coulee Collection, Washington State Archives—Central Region.

86–87. Telegram, Arthur B. Langlie Papers, Washington State Archives, Olympia; *Snoqualmie Valley Record*, microfilm, University of Washington Libraries; poster, Wing Luke Museum of the Asian Pacific Experience; Camp Harmony drawing, UW29396z, Sato Sketchbook, University of Washington Libraries, Special Collections; Kodani letter, Pat Sandbo Collection, Eastside Heritage Center.

88–89. 10% certificate, War Production Board, Arthur B. Langlie Papers, Washington State Archives, Olympia; Brochures, Civilian War Services Subject Files, 1942–44, Office of Civilian Defense (RG 171), National Archives at Seattle; ration book, 3031.3106, Museum of History & Industry.

90. Cook-Martin Collection, Eastside Heritage Center.

91. 29351z, University of Washington Libraries, Special Collections.

92. Benton County Government, Hanford Files, Hanford History, 1938–1995, Washington State Archives—Central Region.

93. SEAPAM files, Special Collections, Seattle Public Library.

94. *Richland Villager*, microfilm, Richland Public Library.

95. Museum of History & Industry.

96. Oral History, *Washington State Legacy Project* www.sos.wa.gov/legacy-project/OralHistories.aspx; brochure, Washington Un-American Activities, Arthur B. Langlie Papers, Washington State Archives, Olympia; Preface, Washington (State) Legislature, Joint Legislative Fact-Finding Committee on Un-American Activities, *First Report, Un-American Activities in Washington State*, Olympia: 1948.

97. Scrapbook, Alaska Steamship Company, Puget Sound Maritime Historical Society.

98. Postcard, Yakima Valley Museum; article and ads, *Goodfruit Grower* (1946–2010), CE32-2-1, Department of Agriculture, Washington State Fruit Commission, Washington State Archives—Central Region.

99. Lake Chelan Historical Society.

100. 1994.4.114, Washington State Historical Society.

101. Kitsap County Sheriff Mug Books, Washington State Archives—Puget Sound Branch.

102. UW29399z, 979.7 Pamphlet File, University of Washington Libraries, Special Collections.

103. Cowlitz County Historical Museum.

104. 2006.53.11, Museum of History & Industry.

105. Museum of History & Industry.

106. Municipality of Metropolitan Seattle, Historical Materials Collection, 1958 Campaign Poster, Washington State Archives—Puget Sound Branch.

107. Century 21 Exposition, World's Fair Commission Correspondence, Washington State Archives—Puget Sound Branch.

108. Ephemera Collection, 9900-01, Box 1 Folder 6, Seattle Municipal Archives.

109. SEAPAM files, Special Collections, Seattle Public Library.

110–111. Century 21 Exposition, Publicity Department Pamphlets and Publications, Washington State Archives—Puget Sound Branch.

112. October 15, 1962, *Seattle Times* online; 29352z and 29353z, Theodore Roethke Collection. University of Washington Libraries, Special Collections; "The Rose," copyright 1963 by Beatrice Roethke, Administratrix of the Estate of Theodore Roethke, from *Collected Poems of Theodore Roethke* by Theodore Roethke. Used by permission of Doubleday, a Division of Random House, Inc.

113. Yakima Valley Museum.

114. Poster from scrapbook, 1951, Box 3 and Poster from scrapbook, 1963, Box 4, Seattle–King County Department of Public Health fluoridation files (Series 254), King County Archives.

115. *Spokane Natural*, Volume 1, Number 8, August 1967, Northwest Museum of Arts and Culture; digitized *Spokane Daily Chronicle* accessible online through Google.

116. Museum of History & Industry.

117. UW29393z and UW29398z, Victor Steinbrueck Papers, University of Washington Libraries, Special Collections.

118–119. Incident Reports, Records of the Public Building Service (RG 121), National Archives at Seattle.

120. D.B. Cooper Case File, Records of the U.S. Attorneys–Seattle (RG 118), National Archives at Seattle.

121. Elevation, Sheet, A-29, Series 497, Kingdome Architectural Records 1972–2000, King County Archives; Stadium 76 logo, drawing and letter, King County Executive John Spellman Stadium Files, Washington State Archives—Puget Sound Region.

122. Oral history, www.sos.wa.gov/legacyproject/OralHistories.aspx; signature, Smith to Betty Coleman, July 20, 1989, Box 4 Folder 6, Sam Smith Departmental Correspondence, Record Series 4682-03, Seattle Municipal Archives; photo, 2001.22.2.01, Black Heritage Society of Washington State.

123. www.boeingimages.com.

124–125. Black and white drawing, Expo '74 Photographs, BB49, Spokane City Planning Department, Washington State Digital Archives and Washington State Archives, Eastern Region; program and color images, Unprocessed Ephemera, Northwest Museum of Arts and Culture.

126. Boldt Decision, U.S. District Court—Western District, Washington State Attorney General, Washington State Archives, Olympia.

127. Mt. St. Helens National Monument Files, Gifford Pinchot National Forest, Records of the Forest Service (RG 95), National Archives at Seattle.

128. MS 212, Northwest Museum of Arts and Culture.

129. Okanogan County Historical Society.

130. State Centennial Planning files, Sue Lean Collection, Washington State Archives, Olympia.

131. Motion 6461 (February 24, 1986), King County Council motion files (Series 306), King County Archives; logo, www.kingcounty.gov/operations/logo.aspx.

132–133. Cartoon, MS 212, Northwest Museum of Arts and Culture; Hanford report and drawings, Benton County Government, Hanford Files, Hanford History, 1938–1995 and Hanford Planning, Clean-up, and Development Background Files, 1979–1997, Washington State Archives—Central Region.

134. State Centennial Planning files, Sue Lean Collection, Washington State Archives, Olympia.

135. Lame Fest: Mudhoney, TAD, and Nirvana, Moore Theatre, Seattle, WA, June 9, 1989. Experience Music Project permanent collection. poster, 1995.91.6, Experience Music Project.

136. http://patft.uspto.gov/ or at any of the federal documents depositories in Washington State.

137. 2007.25.60, Museum of History & Industry.

138–139. Summit Registers, Mount Rainier National Park, Records of the National Park Service (RG 79), National Archives at Seattle.

140. 2001.64, Museum of History & Industry.

141. 2000.12, Museum of History & Industry.

142. I-695, Initiatives, Politics, Washington Secretary of State, Washington State Archives, Olympia.

143. *Goodfruit Grower* (1946–2010), CE32-2-1, Department of Agriculture, Washington State Fruit Commission, Washington State Archives—Central Region. The periodical changed its title from *Goodfruit Grower* to *Good Fruit Grower*.

144. Alweg monorail, Century 21 Exposition, Publicity Department Pamphlets and Publications, Washington State Archives—Puget Sound Branch; map, "Building the Monorail: Seattle Popular Monorail Plan," (2002), SEAPAM, Seattle Public Library.

145. Politics, Washington Secretary of State, Washington State Archives, Olympia.

146. National Remote Sensing Data Archives, USGS Center for Earth Resources Observation and Science, http://eros.usgs.gov/. This image is archived under Satellite Imagery, in the Find Data section.

WITH MANY THANKS TO:

Black Heritage Society of Washington State
Boeing Corporate Archives
Cowlitz County Historical Museum, Kelso
Eastside Heritage Center, Bellevue
Everett Public Library
Experience Music Project, Seattle
Issaquah Historical Society, Issaquah
King County Archives, Seattle
Lake Chelan Historical Society, Chelan
Library of Congress, American Memory Project and Chronicling America
Museum of History & Industry, Seattle
National Archives and Records Administration, Washington, DC
National Archives and Records Administration—Pacific Alaska Region, Seattle
Northwest Museum of Arts and Culture, Spokane
Okanogan County Historical Society, Okanogan
Pend Oreille County Historical Society, Newport
Providence Archives, Seattle
Puget Sound Maritime Historical Society, Seattle
Rainier Valley Historical Society, Seattle
Richland Public Library
Seattle Municipal Archives
Seattle Public Library
Shafer Museum, Winthrop
Stevens County Historical Society, Colville
Swedish-Finn Historical Society, Seattle
Tacoma Public Library
Grant County Historical Society, Ephrata
University of Washington Libraries, Seattle
Washington State Archives
    Central Region—Ellensburg
    Eastern Region—Cheney
    Northwest Region—Bellingham
    Puget Sound Region—Bellevue
    State Archives—Olympia
Washington State Digital Archives
Washington State Historical Society, Tacoma
Washington State Library, Olympia
Whatcom Museum, Bellingham
White River Valley Museum, Auburn
Wing Luke Museum of the Asian Pacific Experience, Seattle
Yakima Valley Libraries
Yakima Valley Museum

Special thanks to the patient archivists at the National Archives and Records Administration, Washington State Archives, King County and Seattle Municipal Archives, and the dozens of libraries and historical societies, who assisted me—thank you from the bottom of my heart. There are nearly one hundred individuals on my thank-you list and I cannot name you all. I will never forget the time and kindness that you showed this fool on her errand. Thank you, and I owe you one.

JUST ONE FINAL REMARK:

Archives matter because documents matter, documents of every sort. What we record, what we write and type, what we draw, what we print, what we microfilm, what we digitize, what we email, what we create that is born-digital in spreadsheets and WAV files—those creations reflect who we were and who we are. My thanks again to the hundreds of archivists and librarians whose careful custody has preserved these documents for us, and for the future. Please don't stop.

Index

151

153

About the Author

LORRAINE MCCONAGHY is the public historian at Seattle's Museum of History & Industry (MOHAI), and she teaches in the Museum Studies graduate program at the University of Washington. She received her PhD in history at the UW in 1991 and has researched and written about Pacific Northwest history ever since. At MOHAI, she curated the core exhibit *Essential Seattle*, as well as *Kalakala: The Prodigal Ship Returns* and *Blue vs. Gray: The Civil War in the Pacific Northwest*. Currently, she is responsible for the research and writing of the core exhibit at the new MOHAI in South Lake Union, opening November 2012. She is a lecturer in the Humanities Washington *Inquiring Mind* series and in MOHAI's outreach program, making presentations on the history of Seattle, King County, and Washington. She is researching the history of the U.S. Navy's Pacific Squadron and Washington Territory during the antebellum, Civil War, and Reconstruction periods, and also working on the Places of Invention programming for the Lemelson Center, of the National Museum of American History. McConaghy is the recipient of the Robert Gray Medal for her distinguished contributions to Pacific Northwest history. She is the author of *Raise Hell and Sell Newspapers! Alden J. Blethen and the Seattle Times* and *Warship Under Sail: The USS Decatur in the Pacific West*.

Henry D Cock
S. S. Ford Junr
Orrington Cushman
Ellis Barnes
m. S. Simmons
Indian Agent

C. H. Mason
Secy. West. Pm
Buy & Shaw
Interpreter

Chaffy Hitchcock
J. M. Goldsborough
Gingelyibbs
John H. Scranton
Henry D Cock
S. S. Ford Junr
Orrington Cushman
Ellis Barnes
m. S. Simmons
Indian Agent

C. H. Mason
Secy. West. Pm
Buy & Shaw
Interpreter

Chaffy Hitchcock
J. M. Goldsborough
Gingelyibbs
John H. Scranton
Henry D Cock
S. S. Ford Junr
Orrington Cushman
Ellis Barnes
m. S. Simmons
Indian Agent

C. H. Mason
Secy. West. Pm
Buy & Shaw
Interpreter

Chaffy Hitchcock
J. M. Goldsborough
Gingelyibbs
John H. Scranton
Henry D Cock
S. S. Ford Junr
Orrington Cushman
Ellis Barnes
m. S. Simmons
Indian Agent

C. H. Mason
Secy. West. Pm
Buy & Shaw
Interpreter

Chaffy Hitchcock
J. M. Goldsborough
Gingelyibbs
John H. Scranton
Henry D Cock
S. S. Ford Junr
Orrington Cushman
m. S. Simmons
Indian Agent

C. H. Mason
Secy. West. Pm
Buy & Shaw
Interpreter

Chaffy Hitchcock
J. M. Goldsborough
Gingelyibbs
John H. Scranton
Henry D Cock
S. S. Ford Junr
Orrington Cushman